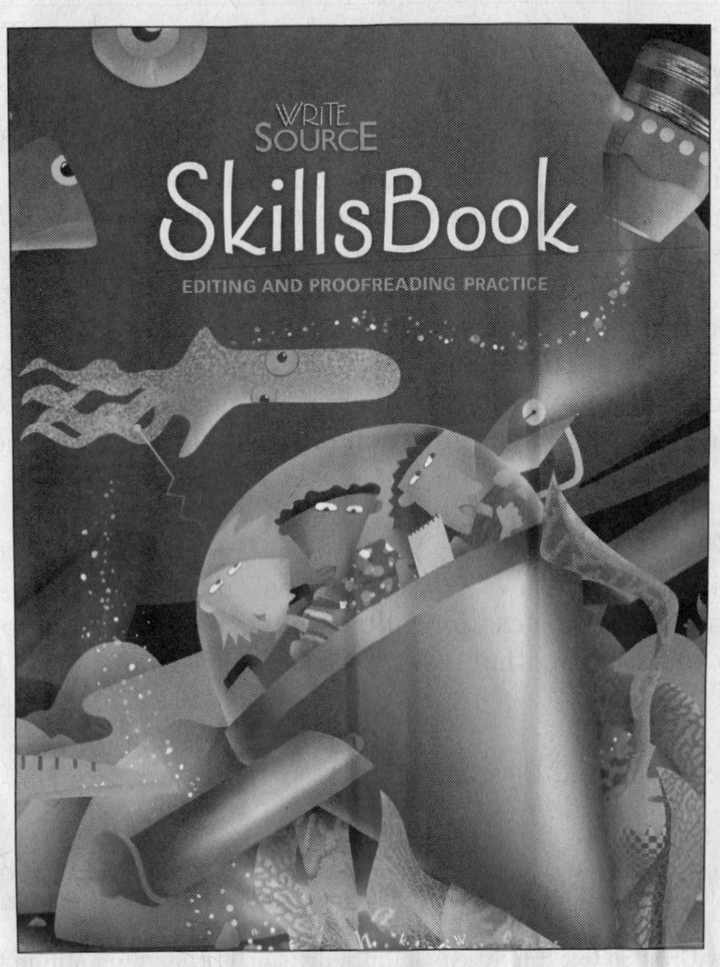

. . . a resource of student activities
to accompany
Write Source

WRITE SOURCE®

GREAT SOURCE EDUCATION GROUP
a division of Houghton Mifflin Company
Wilmington, Massachusetts

A Few Words About the *Write Source SkillsBook*

Before you begin . . .

The *SkillsBook* provides you with opportunities to practice the editing and proofreading skills presented in *Write Source*. That book contains guidelines, examples, and models to help you complete your work in the *SkillsBook*.

Each *SkillsBook* activity includes a brief introduction to the topic and examples illustrating how to complete that activity. You will be directed to the page numbers in the text for additional information and examples. The "Proofreading Activities" focus on punctuation and the mechanics of writing. The "Sentence Activities" provide practice in sentence combining and in correcting common sentence problems. The "Parts of Speech Activities" highlight each of the eight parts of speech.

The Next Step

Most activities include a **Next Step** at the end of the exercise. The purpose of the Next Step is to provide ideas for follow-up work that will help you apply what you have learned to your own writing.

Authors: Pat Sebranek and Dave Kemper

Printed in the United States of America

International Standard Book Number: 978-0-669-50711-9 (student edition)
International Standard Book Number: 0-669-50711-3 (student edition)

1 6 17 18 19 20 - 1689 - 18 17 16 15 14
4 500483540

International Standard Book Number: 0-669-50714-8 (teacher's edition)
3 4 5 6 7 8 9 10 -1689- 09 08

Table of Contents

Proofreading Activities

Marking Punctuation

Editing for Mechanics

Improving Spelling

Using the Right Word

Sentence Activities

Sentence Basics

Sentence Problems

Sentence Variety

Parts of Speech Activities

Nouns

Pronouns

Verbs

Adjectives

Adverbs

Prepositions

Interjections

Conjunctions

Parts of Speech

Proofreading Activities

The activities in this section include sentences that need to be checked for punctuation, mechanics, spelling, or correct word choices. Most of the activities also include helpful *Write Source* references. In addition, the **Next Step** activities encourage follow-up practice of certain skills.

End Punctuation 1

Periods, exclamation points, and question marks are used to signal the end of a sentence. At the same time, the end punctuation marks tell the reader what kind of thought is being expressed in each sentence. (See 579.1, 580.1, and 580.4 in *Write Source* for more information.)

Directions **Put periods, question marks, and exclamation points where they are needed in the following paragraphs. Also supply the needed capital letters at the beginnings of sentences. The first sentence has been done for you.**

Ants are amazing. They survived the extinction of the dinosaurs, and now, millions of years later, there are more ants on the face of the earth than any other creature.

The combined weight of all the ants in the world is about the same as the combined weight of all living humans this is an incredible fact since each ant weighs between 1 and 5 milligrams, or less than one-millionth of a human's weight we are surrounded by 10 thousand trillion of these creatures

Ants are everywhere large-eyed ants dominate the rain forest canopy, while other ants live deep underground aggressive army ants move in formation to hunt and devour animals in their paths some ants take slaves other ants actually tame species, such as aphids, and feed off their secretions

Ants prey upon and transport other insects and spiders into their colonies, burying them and enriching the land they move far more turf than earthworms, mixing vast quantities of nutrients into the soil

Harvester ants alter the environment by transporting seeds into their nests for food they decide which plants will succeed and which will fail by tipping the balance in favor of the plants they prefer to eat

Can you picture an ant gardening some ants create planting beds out of soil, vegetable fibers, and other materials then they plant seeds in the beds as the plants grow, ants feed on them the ant gardens of Central and South America contain many plant species that cannot be found anywhere else

Two ant specialists, Bert Hölldobler and Edward Wilson, studied ants for many years they asked themselves if there might be a good reason for the success of ants they concluded, "Ants, like humans, succeed because they 'talk' so well."

Ants talk by releasing substances that have as much meaning for other ants as words have for people when ants in a colony communicate, their companions cooperate instantly without the colony, ants could not survive

End Punctuation 2

Punctuation controls the movement of your writing. The end punctuation marks—periods, question marks, exclamation points—signal the end of a sentence and help the reader understand what you're trying to say in your writing. (See 579.1, 580.1, 580.4, and 600.1 in *Write Source* for rules and examples.)

Place periods, question marks, and exclamation points where they are needed in the following narrative. Also, make sure the first word in each sentence is capitalized. The first two sentences have been done for you.

We arrived late in the night and pitched our tent in the dim light cast by our camp lanterns we went to bed with no idea where our campsite was located

The next morning, my little brother and I were up as soon as the birds began to chatter we slipped on our clothes and shoes, unzipped the screen door, and stepped outside the others were still nestled in their sleeping bags to our surprise, 100 yards from our door lay a small lake it was a deep green, even in the morning haze on closer inspection, we saw that the lake was covered with a thick blanket of algae at the shoreline, we picked up some rocks and tossed them into the water wherever they landed, dark circles opened up and then closed again

The silence of the morning was broken only by the call of birds, the dripping of trees, and the plops made by our high-arching rocks

Suddenly, we heard a tremendous splash along the shore we wheeled around “look at that” my brother shouted algae was splattered over a 20-foot circle, and ripples were spreading fast

“No fish could have done that,” I said

“Maybe a big turtle” my brother shouted

“Or somebody threw a log,” I said “except nobody else is here”

“Could it be a sea serpent” my brother whispered

“There are no such things,” I informed him

“Oh no then what is that” he pointed to a line of humps moving in the water far across the lake i saw them, too they moved, then disappeared, then reappeared, and then disappeared again

I wanted to believe in creatures like the Loch Ness monster why not my little brother believed with all his heart but I felt too old for that I thought about schools of fish, diving birds, wheels falling from airplanes, meteors from outer space—scientific sorts of things

What made the splash I'll never know but my brother and I will never grow tired of telling the story of the monster in the lagoon—an unsolved mystery in the history of our family camping trips

Next Step Write a journal entry (or a first draft) about a mysterious or scary experience. Don't hold back. Let your reader share in the mystery and excitement. Try starting your story right in the middle of the action. Check your end punctuation when you finish.

Commas Between Items in a Series 1

Commas keep words and ideas from running together in a sentence. They are used between words, phrases, or clauses when there are three or more in a series. Read the following poem aloud.

Without a comma at my command, more
punctuation I would demand.
There'd be no brake to slow the rush, of cursor
crayon pen or brush.
My days of writing soon would end, without that modest little friend
Who slips quietly in between, the words in series long or lean.

Now read it again to figure out where the missing commas should go. (See 582.1 in *Write Source* for more information.)

Directions **Add commas to the series in the sentences below. The first sentence has been done for you.**

1. As we look back on the twentieth century, we should remember, think about, and try to learn from the events that shaped this remarkable period in history.
2. The United States fought in many conflicts during the twentieth century—among them World War I World War II the Korean conflict the war in Vietnam and the Gulf War.
3. Imagine life without antibiotics to fight infections vaccinations to prevent diseases or scanners to diagnose our illnesses.
4. In 1901, a visitor to a foreign city would have experienced strange new foods clothing and languages.

5. Today, in large cities throughout the world, you can find not only the native foods dress and language but also fast-food hamburgers designer jeans and the English language.

6. Do you think that your interests hopes fears beliefs and desires are formed partly by television music and movies?

7. Some countries try to ban foreign entertainment censor radio and television broadcasts destroy historical records or jail protesting citizens in an attempt to control people's thoughts.

8. A history of the twentieth century will cover such topics as climate cycles population growth and urban sprawl.

9. People in the twentieth century created computers radar and penicillin, but they also gave the world hula hoops and foam cups.

10. In the first 25 years after the space age began, people orbited Earth astronauts walked on the moon and space probes studied the solar system.

11. When people study the last decade of the twentieth century, will they include baggy pants nose rings and colored hair as fads or major trends?

Next Step Choose the names of three of your classmates. Write two sentences including all three names. In the first sentence, use just the names themselves in a series. In the second sentence, include each of the names in a phrase or a clause about that person.

Commas Between Items in a Series 2

Commas keep words, phrases, and clauses in a series from running together. Understanding how to use commas is one of the best writing skills you can master. (For more information, see 582.1 in *Write Source.*)

Add commas to the following sentences. Then label the parts of the sentence you've punctuated by writing "W" for word, "P" for phrase, or "C" for clause. The first sentence has been done for you.

1. The U.S. National Park Service exists to protect places of special
W W W W
historical, cultural, scientific, or recreational interest.

2. Kill Devil Hill (site of the Wright brothers' first flight) Manzanar National Historic Site (where Japanese Americans were held during World War II) and Cumberland National Historical Park (site of the Warrior's Path across the Appalachian Mountains) honor events in our nation's history.

3. Recreational parks, like Wolf Trap Farm Park for the Performing Arts, offer art music and theater in a natural, outdoor setting.

4. Yellowstone Glacier Yosemite and Acadia National Parks protect complex ecosystems that might otherwise be lost forever.

5. The increasing number of visitors places great demands on the parks, causing destruction of plant life disruption of animal habitats and pollution of waterways.

6. Even the largest national parks cannot exist as islands in a sea of houses roads and automobiles.

7. Some parks require thousands of acres because elk herds need to migrate from summer to winter pastures wolves need to range over large territories to support their packs and waterfowl need to move freely from one food source to another.

8. The Wilderness Act of 1964 is helping to save our parks by protecting primitive areas re-creating natural habitat and banning development.

Directions **Now it's your turn: Write a paragraph about a park or recreational area you have visited or heard about. Be sure to share what makes the place unique. Include at least one sentence with a series of words, phrases, or clauses.**

Next Step All of the words or phrases you use in a series should be parallel—stated in the same way. Look over your paragraph. Have you used parallel forms in your sentences? Correct any words, phrases, or clauses that need to be changed. (See "Parallelism" on page 559 in *Write Source* for help.)

Other Comma Uses 1

If you want your writing to be clear and easy to understand, you will need to know how to use commas correctly. This activity will help you master three comma uses. (See page 582 in *Write Source* for more information.)

Examples

Commas Separate Items in a Series:
Michael Jordan, Scottie Pippen, and Tony Kukoc started for the Chicago Bulls in the 1997-98 championship season.

Commas Separate Units in a Number:
The Bulls had a sellout streak of 530 games at the 21,500-seat United Center.

Commas Separate Items in a Date or an Address:
On January 30, 1998, I watched the Bulls win at the United Center, which is located at 1901 W. Madison Street, Chicago, Illinois.

Using the rules described above as your guide, add commas as needed to the following sentences.

1. Scottie Pippen overcame back pain a foot injury and contract disputes to play an important part in the Bulls' sixth championship.
2. Scottie Pippen broke Magic Johnson's record of 1724 all-time steals on February 21 1998.
3. Michael Jordan collected 23 points 8 assists 6 rebounds and 3 steals in the All-Star Game.
4. Michael Jordan was named NBA Player of the Week for the weeks of April 5 November 23 and December 21.
5. On February 12 1999 we traveled to Chicago Illinois to see the game against Seattle.

6. My brother mother and three sisters are all Seattle basketball fans.

7. That night, the Chicago team shut down Seattle players Baker Payton and Schrempf.

8. More than 21000 fans attended the game and consumed 14378 hot dogs 10910 bags of peanuts and 18345 soft drinks.

9. This Chicago Bulls team will go down in history as one of the world's greatest after winning six championships in eight years.

10. The Bulls play in the United Center located at 1901 W. Madison Street Chicago Illinois.

11. In 1998, Michael Jordan's annual salary was $33000000 the average NBA player made $2600000 and the minimum salary was $272250.

12. In his first 13 seasons, Michael Jordan played 35887 minutes in 930 games and scored 29277 points.

13. Unlike the NFL the NHL and major league baseball, the NBA had never lost a regular season game because of a labor disagreement until the 1998-99 season.

14. You can contact the commissioner by writing him at the National Basketball Association 645 Fifth Avenue New York New York 10022.

Next Step Write a paragraph of 5 to 6 sentences describing your favorite team—either a professional one or one of your local teams. Try to write some sentences using the rules for commas covered in this exercise. Share your paragraph with a classmate and check each other's work for the correct use of commas.

Other Comma Uses 2

Commas are like the dividers in your school binder. Just as a divider separates your math problems from your science notes, a comma helps you separate one clause or phrase from another, or one adjective from another. (For more information, see 584.1, 586.2, and 590.1 in *Write Source.*)

Examples

Commas Set Off Clauses:

Because Maria practices every day, she is a great snowboarder.

("Because Maria practices every day" is a dependent clause.)

Commas Set Off Phrases:

To compete in the Olympics, Maria must train for years.

("To compete in the Olympics" is an introductory phrase.)

Commas Separate Equal Adjectives:

Many young, athletic skiers are interested in snowboarding.

(The adjectives are *equal* because they could be written as "young" and "athletic.")

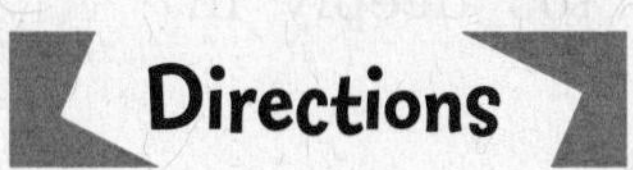

Add commas as necessary to the following sentences. The first sentence has been done for you.

1. Because snowboarding is easy to learn, it is very popular.
2. Although snowboarding is sometimes compared to skateboarding snowboarding is more like surfing.
3. Yesterday, several snowboarders tried racing through icy rutted snow.
4. If you are interested in trying snowboarding you should get the right equipment.
5. After testing out lots of boards Karlowe decided to get a freestyle board.
6. Because it is the shortest and widest of snowboards the freestyle board makes tricks easier to do.

7. A *halfpipe* is a long deep snow trench that snowboarders use to do flips and jumps.

8. Snowboards were invented by a creative East Coast surfer who got the idea by sliding over fresh deep snow on a cafeteria tray.

9. Because snowboarders can get very wet and cold they wear multiple layers of clothing.

10. Snowboarding can be done anywhere that skiing is done except on flat cross-country trails.

11. Snowboarding equipment includes a freestyle or slalom board, bindings, and thick chunky boots.

12. When first learning to snowboard you have to decide to lead with your left foot or lead with your right.

13. If you catch the front or rear edge of your snowboard too deeply in the snow you may crash.

14. After finding a great place to board just strap yourself to the board and surf down the hill.

15. If you are excited about trying snowboarding you can rent some basic used equipment and ride the nearest halfpipe.

Next Step In a paragraph, describe why you like (or don't like) snowboarding. Try to use introductory phrases and clauses in your writing. Remember to separate each introductory phrase or clause from the rest of the sentence with a comma.

Commas to Set Off Nonrestrictive Phrases and Clauses 1

Let's practice punctuating **nonrestrictive** phrases and clauses, including appositives. The first step is to identify the phrase or clause as nonrestrictive—or unnecessary to the basic meaning of the sentence. The next step is to set off the nonrestrictive phrase or clause with commas. (Review the differences between restrictive and nonrestrictive below and also see 584.1 in *Write Source.*)

Examples

Restrictive:
The man who made Silly Putty became a millionaire.
(The information in the clause "who made Silly Putty" is needed to understand the sentence.)

Nonrestrictive:
Silly Putty, a glob of stretchy goo, was first called Nutty Putty.
(The information in the phrase "a glob of stretchy goo" is not needed to understand the sentence.)

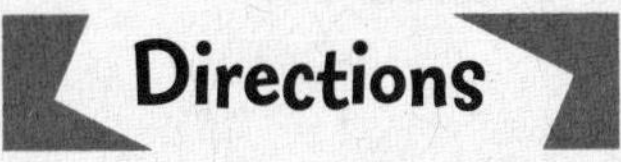

Add commas as necessary to the following sentences. The first sentence has been done for you.

1. Silly Putty, originally known as Nutty Putty, was discovered in 1943 by James Wright.
2. James Wright an engineer for General Electric accidentally made Nutty Putty in his laboratory.
3. James Wright thought that Nutty Putty which is made of boric acid and silicone oil had no practical uses.
4. Peter Hodgson an unemployed advertiser found Nutty Putty in a toy store.

5. Hodgson called it Silly Putty and put it into small, plastic eggs that he sold for a dollar each.

6. The product that no one wanted made Hodgson a millionaire.

7. Silly Putty which became popular in the 1950s was pressed against comics and then stretched to make crazy impressions.

8. Soon kids who owned this stretchy goo realized that Silly Putty could also bounce very high.

9. In 1968, the astronauts who traveled on Apollo 8 carried Silly Putty into space to fight boredom and to fasten down tools during weightlessness.

10. In 1990, Binney and Smith Inc. the makers of Silly Putty added fluorescent colors.

11. Silly Putty which is now more than 50 years old is still a very popular toy.

12. A person who has a great imagination can think of new uses for ordinary products.

13. The Columbus Zoo which is in Ohio used Silly Putty to make plaster casts of gorillas' hands and feet.

Next Step Copy three sentences from this activity that contain a nonrestrictive phrase or clause. Then revise each sentence by crossing out the phrase or clause and substituting your own words. Be sure that the phrase or clause you add is nonrestrictive. Share your writing with a classmate.

Commas to Set Off Nonrestrictive Phrases and Clauses 2

Let's try punctuating more sentences that include restrictive and nonrestrictive information. Remember that nonrestrictive or unnecessary phrases and clauses are set off with commas, but restrictive phrases and clauses are not set off with commas. (For more information, see 584.1 in *Write Source*.)

Add a comma before and after the nonrestrictive information. (Not all sentences need commas.) The first sentence has been done for you.

1. My youngest brother, Arturo, has a pet iguana named Felix.
2. Kids who want exotic pets must spend a lot of time learning how to take care of them.
3. Samir's parrot Maurice loves to mimic phone conversations and country singers.
4. The iguana that Joe owns eats both plants and animals.
5. The scarlet macaw a popular pet gets sick easily.
6. Cockatoos that mimic human speech are popular cage birds.
7. One of the largest cockatoos the great palm has black feathers and patches of bright red skin on its cheeks.
8. All cockatoos have feathered crests which they can raise or flatten.
9. The tarantula a long-legged, hairy spider is found in warm areas.
10. Tarantulas use their big fangs to inject venom which can be deadly into their victims.

11. The miniature potbellied pig one of the smartest exotic pets is easy to train.

12. Pigs that wallow in the mud are trying to stay cool and to protect themselves from lice and other bugs.

13. The anaconda a semiaquatic snake is found in Central America and South America.

14. Anacondas which eat birds and small animals make unusual pets.

15. The giant anaconda that lives in our zoo is already 35 years old.

16. Levi wants to buy the boa that he saw advertised in the classified ads.

17. His mother who is afraid of snakes wants him to buy a macaw.

18. Most lizards except the desert iguana sleep during the hottest part of the day.

19. Exotic pets that are well cared for may live for many years.

20. Every year veterinarians must find new homes for exotic pets that have become too big or too dangerous for their owners.

21. Kids who want exotic pets must remember that these pets require a lot of care.

22. Owning an anaconda or a black widow spider both dangerous animals is not a good idea.

Next Step Write three sentences of your own that contain nonrestrictive infomation. Ask a classmate to place the commas in the correct places. Try to stump your classmate with creative sentences.

Commas with Interruptions, Direct Address, and Interjections

Commas sometimes separate the unnecessary parts of sentences from the necessary parts. For example, when a word or phrase or clause is not necessary to the basic meaning of a sentence, that word or phrase or clause is separated from the rest of the sentence by a comma or by commas. **Interruptions, nouns of direct address**, or **interjections** are considered nonessential and are separated from the main sentence with commas. (For more information, see 584.3, 588.2, and 588.3 in *Write Source.*)

Examples

"Didn't you swim with dolphins, Hillary?"

"Yeah, I also swam near a shark, believe it or not, off the Florida Keys."

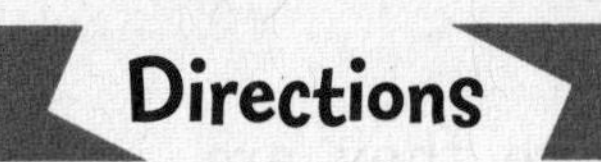

Add commas wherever they are needed in the sentences that follow. The first sentence has been done for you.

1. Of course, just the thought of a shark, as we all know, sends shivers down most swimmers' spines.
2. Contrary to popular belief though sharks rarely attack people.
3. "Simply stated Bill humans have not swum in the oceans long enough for sharks to adapt to hunting humans."
4. Many myths most of them untrue have developed about sharks.
5. Some people think even though it's not true that sharks must swim continuously so that they don't sink.

6. Not surprisingly this belief is based on the fact that unlike other fish sharks do not have a swim bladder filled with air to help them stay afloat in the water.

7. A shark's huge liver almost 75 percent of its body weight contains enough fat to make the fish float.

8. Without a fish's air-filled swim bladder you see deepwater sharks can move rapidly from the depths to the surface without decompressing.

9. Sharks unchanged in the last 70 million years are seldom seen in fossils.

10. Fossils are rare unfortunately because sharks have skeletons made of cartilage like the framework of your nose and ears instead of bone.

11. Some baby sharks are born live while others hatch from eggs deposited in pods known believe it or not as "mermaids' purses."

12. Just imagine sharks must grow for about 15 years before they are mature enough to reproduce.

13. "Yes Jamal sharks need protection since they are being killed more quickly than they can replace themselves."

Next Step Write a letter to send to your local newspaper, or to share with your class, about a topic you know or care about. Remember to check your facts before sending or sharing your letter.

Commas to Set Off Explanatory and Appositive Phrases

Commas are used to set off explanatory phrases from the rest of the sentence. Explanatory, or nonrestrictive, phrases contain information that is *not* necessary to the basic meaning of the sentence. That's why they are set off by commas. (For more information, see 586.1 and 588.4 in *Write Source*.)

Examples

Commas Set Off Explanatory Phrases:
The Grand Canyon, located in northwestern Arizona, is an incredible place.

Commas Set Off Nonrestrictive Appositive Phrases:
Bob, my classmate, visited the Grand Canyon.

Directions **Add commas to the following sentences as needed. The first sentence has been done for you.**

1. Bob and Paola, Bob's neighbor, took a trip to the Grand Canyon last summer.
2. The Grand Canyon which contains buttes, mesas, and valleys is an awesome place to visit.
3. The boys rented burros small donkeys to use when traveling down the trails to the bottom of the canyon.
4. Their guide Raoul warned them that they should dress in layers because the temperature changes quickly in the canyon.
5. The temperature at the bottom of the canyon even in the fall can be very warm.

6. The two friends both camping fanatics wanted to set up camp at the bottom of the canyon.

7. They carried supplies including tents and sleeping bags on the backs of their burros.

8. Bob's parents Phil and Maria Magrath stayed at the top of the canyon.

9. The parents agreed after a lot of persuading to let the boys join a camping group headed to the bottom of the canyon.

10. The camping trip four days and three nights was one the boys will never forget.

11. The campers left from the canyon's south rim 7,000 feet above sea level and rode their burros down the steep trail.

12. The boys' burros named Pancho and Cisco were very surefooted on the narrow trail that wound 5,000 feet down to the Colorado River.

13. The boys had to keep their burros very close together, and sometimes the burros letting others pass stepped right near the edge of the trail.

14. Temperatures reached 100° F which is 38° C so the boys had to drink a gallon of water each day to avoid dehydrating.

15. The boys were on the lookout for a special type of snake the Grand Canyon rattlesnake that blends into the canyon's pink sandstone.

Next Step Think about a park or campsite that you know well, and imagine camping there with a friend. Then write a paragraph or two describing your experience. Ask a classmate to check your writing for correct comma usage. Then share your writing with the class.

Commas in Compound Sentences

One way to join two independent clauses is to connect them with a comma and a coordinating conjunction (*and, but, or, nor, for, so, yet*). Knowing that you can combine simple sentences in this way will help you to edit more effectively. Also, using this technique will help you to create smoother transitions and more interesting sentences. (See 590.2 in *Write Source* for more information.)

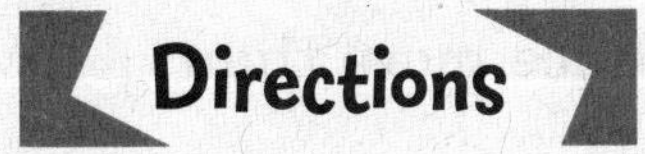

Combine each of the following groups of sentences by using a comma and a coordinating conjunction. Avoid creating comma splices, which result from combining two sentences without a conjunction. The first sentence has been done for you.

1. Blue whales are the largest living creatures. Tortoises have the longest life span.

Blue whales are the largest living creatures, but tortoises have the longest life span.

2. Some swifts and falcons can travel at more than 200 miles per hour. Only hummingbirds can fly backward.

3. Amazon ants are fierce. Fire ants are even fiercer and have been known to sting birds and other larger animals.

4. Most mammals see color as shades of gray. Some apes and monkeys see all the colors.

5. A centipede should have 100 legs, according to its name. Some centipedes have more than 250 pairs of legs.

6. Mammals have red blood. Insects have yellow blood.

7. Dogs can produce about 10 different sounds. Cats can produce more than 100 vocal sounds.

8. An owl cannot move its eyes. An owl must move its whole head to look in different directions.

9. Elephant seals can stay underwater for 30 minutes. They can dive to depths of more than 500 feet.

Next Step Write a paragraph about a particular type of plant or animal that interests you. Try to use several compound sentences in your writing. Share your paragraph with a classmate.

Comma Rules

Of all of the punctuation marks, the one that has the most uses—and probably causes the most confusion—is the comma. *Write Source* covers many different rules for using commas. (For more information see pages 582–590 in *Write Source.*)

Place commas correctly in each sample sentence. Then write the rule that applies to the comma usage. Use *Write Source* to do this exercise. The first sentence has been done for you.

1. My favorite foods are hamburgers, french fries, and pizza.

Rule: ***Commas are used between words, phrases, or clauses in a series.***

2. Mom must have told me at least 1 0 0 0 0 0 1 times to improve my diet.

Rule: ____

3. On February 1 2004 we will be moving to Boston Massachusetts.

Rule: ____

4. "I'm sure " said Dad "that Boston has some good pizza parlors."

Rule: ____

5. We can't however stay very long.

Rule: ____

6. Yes we'll be there on time.

Rule: ______________________________

____

7. Dad is that all you think I'm worried about?

Rule: ______________________________

____

8. The two friends love to go golfing and they are working to qualify for the state tournament next year.

Rule: ______________________________

____

9. My uncle beamed as he took hold of the large shining trophy.

Rule: ______________________________

____

10. My uncle an expert angler won the fishing contest.

Rule: ______________________________

____

11. Uncle Josh who had traveled 600 miles to participate was very glad he had entered the fishing contest.

Rule: ______________________________

____

____

Comma Review

Directions **After reviewing the comma rules in the previous exercises, place commas correctly in the following sentences. (See pages 582–590 in *Write Source* for more information.)**

1. A group of geese is a *gaggle* but it is more commonly called a flock.

2. A *clip joint* is a shop store or other place of business where customers are overcharged.

3. *Acrophobia* is the fear of heights *claustrophobia* is the fear of enclosed spaces and *hydrophobia* is the fear of water.

4. Abraham Lincoln was born on February 12 1809 on a farm near Hodgenville Kentucky.

5. Mr. Lincoln served as president of the United States from March 4 1861 to April 15 1865.

6. On June 3 1979 more than 140000000 gallons of oil spilled from an oil well in the Gulf of Mexico.

7. Mark's new address is 310 Greens Drive Boston Massachusetts 02109.

8. Send your requests to the *Daily Post* 211 Main Street Willowlane Missouri 64402.

9. "Did you know" asked Dan "that London Bridge is no longer in London?"

10. "Sue these are my parents."

11. Mr. Dobson our English teacher is out with the flu.

12. Sliding into first base I scraped my elbow raw.

Directions Place commas correctly in the following sentences. (Refer to pages 582–590 in *Write Source* if necessary.)

1. "Dad here are the good seats we've been telling you about."
2. "Wow" said Chris "these are great!"
3. The usher a young man with a beard heard him and smiled.
4. Dad took orders and went to get sodas popcorn and pretzels.
5. The attendance by the way turned out to be more than 42000.
6. The names and locations of Caroline Adams M.D. and Samuel Cline M.D. were posted on signs near the stage in case of emergencies.
7. We saw Miss Daniels our neighbor at the concert.
8. The music which sounded perfect from our seats carried out to the far ends of the stadium.
9. The concert was fantastic and the crowd loving it clapped and screamed loudly.
10. Boy it was hard to believe I would enjoy the same music as my grandpa a teenager in the '70s.
11. For a bunch of old guys the band called the Rolling Stones really rocked.
12. Everybody loved it when Mick Jagger the Stones' lead singer strutted across the stage.
13. The Stones' encore included "As Tears Go By" "Angie" and "Get Off Of My Cloud" but they didn't play "Ruby Tuesday."
14. "This concert was a lot mellower than the Stones' concert at Altamont on December 6 1969" Grandpa said.

Semicolons and Colons

A **semicolon** is sometimes used in place of a period or in place of a comma and a conjunction. A semicolon signals that the ideas in the two independent clauses are similar in thought or in style. (*He came; he conquered.*)

A **colon,** on the other hand, mainly calls the readers' attention to what comes after the colon, whether it be a list or a key word. (For more information, see pages 594 and 596 in *Write Source.*)

Examples

Semicolons Join Independent Clauses:
My brother listens to punk rock; I listen to country music.
(Instead of a comma and a conjunction, a semicolon joins the two independent clauses.)

Semicolons Join Independent Clauses Connected by a Conjunctive Adverb:
Margarita listens to the Beatles; however, she also likes jazz music.
(A semicolon joins the two independent clauses with the conjunctive adverb "however.")

Colons Introduce a List:
Motown Records has recorded many great artists: Stevie Wonder, Diana Ross, Smokie Robinson, the Temptations, and the Four Tops.

Colons Separate a Word for Emphasis:
Most record companies are motivated by the same thing: money.

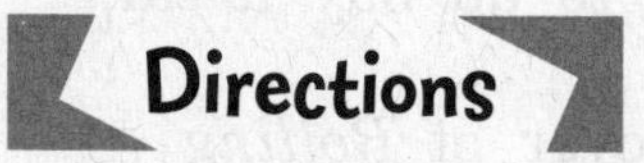

Add semicolons and colons to the following sentences as needed. The first sentence has been done for you.

1. My friends and I want to start our own band; however, we can't agree on a name for it.

2. I think the name Purple Watermelons is cool Yuri thinks that it's too weird.

3. Our band wants to get some experience playing in public as a result, we're willing to play anywhere.

4. We play many different kinds of music however, we don't play anything very well.

5. My mom thinks there's only one word to describe our band loud.

6. Umberto plays the following instruments saxophone, guitar, trumpet, electric bass, synthesizer, and drums.

7. Last week we played at the Summerdale Senior Center they didn't like our music.

8. We try to play all kinds of music folk, punk, rap, and country.

9. There is one thing that separates good bands from poor ones practice.

10. My friends and I dream of recording a hit song we want to be big stars.

11. We practice in our garage many famous musicians started out by playing in unique places garages, attics, churches, and parks.

12. We experiment with new styles we have a country-pop song, a folk-punk song, and a swing-rock song.

13. Our best gig so far was the kindergarten graduation we really had those kids rocking.

14. If we do become stars, there are many things I want to do buy a car, meet other stars, and get our band's picture on the cover of *Rolling Stone.*

15. We even have the title of our first album picked out *Fame.*

Next Step Write a paragraph about a dream you have for your future—what you hope to do when you are an adult. Describe that dream in a paragraph using the rules for semicolons and colons. Share your writing with a classmate.

Punctuating Dialogue

Talking is so easy that you don't have to think about it. You just . . . talk. But recording "talk" on paper is another matter entirely—one that can be a lot of work. There are definite rules to follow regarding the use of quotation marks, commas, end marks, and capital letters. (See 598.1, 598.2, and 600.1 in *Write Source* for more information.)

Example

"When will we leave for camp?" asked Todd.
(The *question mark* is placed inside the quotation marks because the quotation is a question.)

Punctuate the following dialogue with quotation marks, commas, and end marks. The first sentence has been done for you.

"All aboard, Scouts!" said Counselor Dave as he climbed into the bus. Are you men prepared to camp in the Sonora Desert tonight

Not yet Dave shouted Andy We still need to buy some sandpaper

Why do you need sandpaper asked the puzzled counselor

Andy grinned We're going to need a map when we drive through the desert

As the bus pulled up to the campground, Counselor Dave shouted The last man off this bus is a rotten egg

Excuse me Counselor said Andy I can't get down off the bus

Why not asked the counselor What is the problem

Everyone knows you can only get *down* from a goose Andy laughed

The next morning Counselor Dave rubbed his aching back and yawned I didn't sleep a wink in my tent, so I traded with Counselor Ted. His tent wasn't any better

Andy laughed and said No wonder. You were just too tense, trying to sleep in two tents.

Next Step In the space above, write a short dialogue with a partner. Take turns writing, just as if you were talking.

Quotation Marks and Italics

Quotation marks are used to punctuate titles of shorter works. Titles of longer works are italicized. (If you are handwriting the title of a longer work, you should underline it.) For more information about italics and quotation marks, refer to 600.3 and 602.3 in *Write Source*.

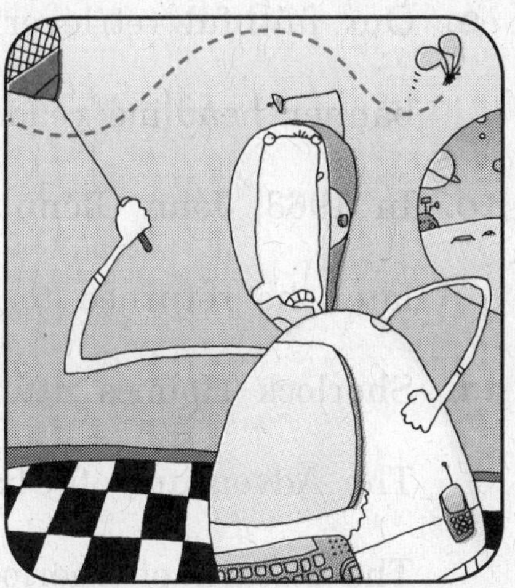

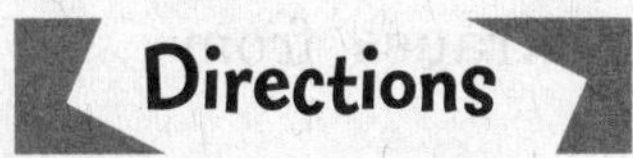

Punctuate the following sentences. Remember that periods and commas are always placed inside quotation marks. The first sentence has been done for you.

1. In the <u>Utne Reader</u> magazine article "How to Future-Proof Your Life," the author says you should pack lightly.
2. A burglary at the Watergate Hotel in Washington, D.C., was reported in the Washington Post and recorded in the book All the President's Men.
3. Two books I like are Are You My Mother? and The Cat in the Hat.
4. As Titanic was sinking, the band played Nearer, My God, to Thee.
5. A moving song, The Circle of Life, from the movie The Lion King is inspired by African drumming.
6. Online magazines, or interactive magazines, such as Digital Animators, appeal to readers who would rather surf the Internet than browse through libraries.
7. Melville's novel Moby Dick is famous for its whaling lore, such as the chapter titled Scrimshander.
8. Please turn up the volume so we can hear the song Octopus's Garden.

9. Our faithful retriever wouldn't bring in the newspaper because the banner headline read Man Bites Dog.

10. In 1963, John Glenn blasted into space in Friendship 7, and 35 years later, he returned to space aboard the space shuttle Discovery.

11. Sherlock Holmes utters the classic line, By Jove, Watson, I've got it! in The Adventure of Charles August Milverton, a story from the book The Return of Sherlock Holmes.

12. When You Say Nothing at All was a big hit for Alison Krauss from her Alison Krauss and Union Station Live CD.

13. Many newspapers, including the New York Times, Chicago Tribune, and San Jose Mercury News, have their own Web sites.

14. Humphrey Bogart never said, "Play it again, Sam," in the movie Casablanca, a film based on a play called Everybody Comes to Rick's.

15. The school newspaper, the Yorkville Yacker, reviewed the movie Finding Nemo in an article entitled Fishy Fun.

16. The musical group Chicago, the musical play Chicago, and the poem Chicago by Robert Frost are all named after the Illinois city.

Next Step On your own paper, write three sentences. In the first sentence, include the title of a song. In the second one, include the title of a poem, and in the third one, include the title of an article in a newspaper. When you have finished, check your work to be sure you have used italics and quotation marks correctly.

Italics and Parentheses

Italics are like flashing lights. They catch your attention right away because they look different than the regular type on the page. Italics alert readers to titles, foreign words, and words that are being used in a special way.

Parentheses separate words or phrases added to a sentence to make it clearer. They are really a lot like commas and dashes because they help prevent ideas from getting jumbled together. We use parentheses instead of commas and dashes when we want less emphasis on the separated material. (*Write Source* explains the uses of italics and parentheses in more detail at 602.3–602.5, and 612.4.)

Examples

Italics in Titles:
The River **is one of my favorite adventure books.**

Italics for Foreign Words:
Orcinus orca **is the Latin name for killer whale.**

Italics for Special Uses:
Try to say ***rubber baby buggy bumpers*** **five times fast.**

Parentheses for Added Information:
The author (Gary Paulsen) is a favorite of kids.

Directions **Add underlining (for italics) or parentheses to the following sentences. The first sentence has been done for you.**

1. I have such a hard time saying the word minimum.
2. S. E. Hinton wrote The Outsiders when she was 16 years old.
3. The article on skydiving was in last month's issue of Sports Illustrated.
4. Our house in Grand Marais actually the north shore of Lake Superior is really a cabin.
5. This winter I saw Lord of the Rings: The Return of the King at a movie theater downtown.

6. The Latin name for one of the largest dinosaurs is Tyrannosaurus Rex.

7. Everyone thought Titanic was an unsinkable ship.

8. The New York Times published an article about kids starting their own businesses.

9. What is the French word for love?

10. How many i's are there in the word Mississippi?

11. You should order at least six dozen 72 barbecue buns for the party.

12. The tongue twister Peter Piper is harder to say than the tongue twister she sells seashells.

13. With his new braces, Paul found it hard to say s's and th's.

14. He rode his bike actually a moped back and forth to school.

15. Have you read The Hatchet, another book by Gary Paulsen?

16. If you switch the letters r and d in the word read, you get dear.

17. Parentheses those curvy brackets are always used in a pair to set off words in a sentence.

18. CD's compact discs replaced magnetic tapes as the main format for storing recorded music.

19. The Spanish word hola and the Italian phrase buòn giorno mean the same thing hello.

Next Step Write a paragraph about your favorite book or movie. Describe it using details that would convince someone else to read the book or see the movie you are describing. What made that book or movie really interesting? Use italics and parentheses whenever necessary in this paragraph. Share your paragraph with the class.

Apostrophes 1

Apostrophes are used to form contractions and to show ownership or possession. (See 604.1, 604.4, and 606.1–606.4 in *Write Source* for more information about apostrophes.)

Examples

To Form Contractions:

Wouldn't riding a unicycle be fun?
(would + not = wouldn't)

To Show Possession:

A unicycle's wheel is small.

Directions **For each of the underlined words below, write "C" if an apostrophe is used correctly, add apostrophes to the words that need them, and correct any misplaced apostrophes. The first two sentences have been done for you.**

Paula loves to ride her friend's unicycle. She didn't take long to learn, and she doesnt worry about falling. A unicycle is recognized easily by it's single wheel. Paula's friend received his unicycle from his brother-in-law; its seat is mounted on a pole 20 feet high. Naturally, a unicycles' pedals must be up near the seat. Paula's friend's vehicle is not your usual, run-of-the-mill unicycle. Pumping a unicycle is hard, sweaty work, so theres a fan installed on the 20-foot pole with a generator attached to the wheel's hub. Isn't Paula's friends' riding machine a sight to see? Now they cant wait to try out the brother's-in-law new toy—a *miniature* unicycle.

Apostrophes 2

By now, you know that apostrophes are used to form contractions and to show possession, but they can do other things, too. In this activity, you'll discover some other ways you can use apostrophes. (See 604.2, 604.3, and 606.5 in *Write Source* for more information.)

Examples

In Place of Omitted Letters or Numbers:

In the summer of '98, we rode 16 rockin' roller coasters.

To Form Plurals:

Be sure to cross your t's and dot your i's.

To Express Time or Amount:

My dad took a week's vacation so that he could come with us.

Directions **Add at least one apostrophe to each of the following sentences. You will need to form contractions in some sentences.**

1. Marcel could not wait to ride the Son of Beast, the fastest wooden roller coaster in the world.
2. He saved a months worth of allowance for the class of 05 trip.
3. The figure 8s on this roller coaster made it especially scary.
4. Lionel does not know whether he should try the Hercules or Batman.
5. Its hard to imagine that either could be scarier than the Desperado.
6. People sat in rows of 2s and 3s in the hanging roller coaster.
7. Tomorrows rides will be even more amazing than todays rides.
8. They will be faster, bigger, and more daring.
9. Whos going to be brave enough to try these new roller coasters?

Next Step Write a journal entry (or a first draft of a story) about a special vehicle in your life. Make sure that you use apostrophes correctly in your writing. Share your results.

Apostrophes 3

Apostrophes can be used in your writing to show possession—to say, “Hey, that belongs to me!” (See 604.4 and 606.1–606.4 in *Write Source* for more details about how to use apostrophes to show possession.)

Examples

Singular Possessives:

Cedar Point’s Mean Streak roller coaster is one of the world’s longest wooden coasters.

Plural Possessives:

The visitors’ hearts raced as they plunged down the coaster hills.

Shared Possession:

Latoya, Eli, and Gabriel’s favorite roller coaster is the Wild Thing at Valleyfair.
Latoya’s, Eli’s, and Gabriel’s favorite snacks are different.

Possessives in Compound Nouns:

My sister-in-law’s biggest fear is falling out of a roller coaster.

Possessives with Indefinite Pronouns:

Everyone’s hands grab the safety bar during loops.

Directions **In the following sentences, add an apostrophe where needed to show possession. But be careful—not every sentence needs an apostrophe. The first sentence has been done for you.**

1. The earliest roller coasters’ tracks were made from cut lumber and tree trunks.
2. The first roller coasters were made in Russia in the fifteenth century.
3. Childrens lives were often in danger on those early roller coasters.
4. The worlds first hanging roller coaster appeared in 1981 in Cincinnati, Ohio.
5. In July 2003, the worlds tallest and fastest hanging roller coaster was the Top Thrill Dragster.

6. The Top Thrill Dragsters fastest speed is 120 miles per hour.

7. Its features include diving loops, rolls, and high-speed spirals.

8. My sister-in-laws scariest ride was on the Thunder Run at Kentuckys Six Flags.

9. Roller coasters safety rules protect the lives of their passengers.

10. Jaccos, Ruths, and Tobies families spend the summer going from one amusement park to the next.

11. The worlds first thrill ride to reach 100 miles per hour was Dreamworlds Tower of Terror.

12. The 8,133-foot Steel Dragon 2000 is Japans longest steel roller coaster.

13. The Beast is everyones favorite wooden roller coaster.

14. This years most popular roller coaster was the Desperado at Buffalo Bills Resort in Nevada.

15. The countrys first steel roller coaster was Disneylands Matterhorn Mountain, which opened in 1959.

16. Coney Islands Wonder Wheel combines a Ferris wheels circular path with a roller coasters thrills.

17. Our family rated ten roller coasters, and my two brothers top choice was Apollos Chariot.

Next Step In a paragraph describe your favorite amusement park ride. Ask a classmate to check your writing for correct use of possessive apostrophes.

Hyphens

Hyphens can be used to divide words at the end of a line and to form compound words. It might seem that hyphens have two opposite purposes; but really, hyphens have a single purpose: to make your writing clearer. (Refer to 608.2–608.4 and 610.2 in *Write Source* for more information.)

Examples

To Make a Compound Word:
My thirteen-year-old sister is very good at Frisbee golf.

To Create New Words:
The self-taught musician started his own band.

Between Numbers in a Fraction or a Compound Number:
Would twenty-two people each drink one-half cup of eggnog?

To Join Letters and Words:
The boomerang, a V-shaped stick, was sold by Wham-O Manufacturing.

Add hyphens to the following sentences as needed. The first sentence has been done for you.

1. My brother-in-law owns nine Frisbees and thirty-two hula hoops.
2. My great uncle was a friend of the Frisbee's inventors.
3. These self employed inventors also created popular toys like boomerangs and slingshots.
4. Many ever popular products were made by long forgotten inventors.
5. The can opener was invented in 1858, but a more user friendly version was made in 1870.
6. Blue jeans, the all American pants, were invented by a canvas salesperson from San Francisco during the gold rush of the 1850s.

7. By inventing these basic all around pants, Levi Strauss created a new industry.

8. Blue jeans, now a world famous product, were first made out of canvas.

9. In 1916, Garrett Augustus Morgan was given a medal for his safety hood invention, which led to the development of the gas mask.

10. Use of the just invented gas mask saved the lives of three fourths of the workers in a tunnel explosion that year.

11. One of the ex directors of the American Red Cross was Dr. Charles Drew.

12. Out of work people sometimes become great inventors.

13. One of the most well known inventors was Alexander Graham Bell.

14. It took many years of trial and error research to invent the X ray machine.

15. Forty one out of sixty eight people agreed that most inventions are made from one tenth inspiration and nine tenths perspiration.

16. If you have an idea for a super duper invention, you could possibly become a self made millionaire.

Next Step Invent a game that you could play with an everyday product found in your home. Then write a paragraph or two explaining how to play the game. Ask a classmate to read your writing and check for correct use of hyphens.

Hyphens and Dashes

Hyphens connect words, numbers, and letters. **Dashes** can add interruptions, information, or emphasis to your writing. Though dashes can be an effective writing tool, don't overuse them! (See pages 608, 610, and 612.1–612.3 in *Write Source* for more about dashes and hyphens.)

Examples

Hyphens:

Being a juggler isn't an average nine-to-five job.
(The hyphens turn the words "nine to five" into a single-thought adjective.)

Dashes:

Look out—that puddle is two feet deep!
(The dash and following text add emphasis and information to the warning.)

Punctuate the following sentences correctly. The first sentence has been done for you.

1. That's not your run-of-the-mill slam dunk.
2. Your brother in law really knows how to fix cars.
3. My great grandfather is 99 today.
4. There's only one sport swimming I've ever really enjoyed.
5. Can we make a U turn and go back to that gas station?
6. No one and I mean no one may leave this room.
7. The woman slipped on the ice covered sidewalk an accident waiting to happen.
8. Arlo Hale is the president elect of the Nottingham Running Club.
9. The blue and white striped bench had a wet paint sign on it.
10. I could eat only three fourths of the big slice of strawberry rhubarb pie.

Dashes

Dashes set off parts of a sentence or show a sudden break in the flow of a sentence. They create pauses in your writing that are a bit stronger and more dramatic than comma pauses. Use them sparingly in formal writing. (See 612.1–612.3 in *Write Source* for more information.)

Examples

To Indicate a Sudden Break:
Never—and I mean never—has a toy sold as well as the hula hoop.

To Emphasize a Certain Word, a Series of Words, a Phrase, or a Clause:
The hula hoop—an Australian invention—was first sold in the United States.

To Indicate Interrupted Speech:
I wanted to tell you that—well, that—I lost your hula hoop.

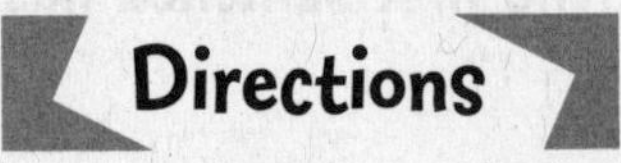

Add dashes to the following sentences as needed. The first sentence has been done for you.

1. Both Frisbees and hula hoops were popular—very popular—in the 1950s.
2. Frisbees, Silly Putty, yo-yos all of these have become classic toys.
3. The first hula hoops cost only $1.98 an unbelievable bargain!
4. Between 60 and 100 million hula hoops an incredible number were sold in just a few months.
5. Last week no, let me see was it yes, last week I bought a hula hoop.
6. The hula hoop was named after a very popular Hawaiian dance the hula.
7. In the 1940s, students at Yale University tossed around pie platters from the local bakery William R. Frisbie's Bakery between classes.
8. The students were never as you might imagine given credit for their invention.

Punctuation Review 1

Directions **Proofread the paragraphs below. Draw a line through any mark of punctuation or word that is used incorrectly; add any needed punctuation or capital letters. (For more information see pages 579–612 in *Write Source.*) The first two sentences have been done for you.**

Picture a New England beach in autumn. The sky is clear; the sun warms your face. The green sea has washed ashore almost 100 of it's most magnificent creatures whales to die. A biologist walks among the bloating bodies of the whales and he is clearly puzzled.

Mass whale suicides, or "strandings" as they are called, occur year after year. Many people have tried to understand these unusual deaths, even Aristotle the ancient Greek, philosopher thought about the whales deaths. Although he decided the whales may indeed be killing themselves modern biologists are not so easily convinced."

One researcher points out that the whales may have once been land dwelling animals. He thinks the whales may simply be remembering their ancient roots, and beaching themselves to "go home." This habit however would have put the whale close to extinction years ago so the idea doesn't make much sense.

A newer theory suggests that the whales blindly follow their food supplies, into shallow water. For example they may swim after a shoal of squid quickly eat their dinner and then find themselves too close to the shore.

Another theory says that whales follow the earths magnetic forces as though they were following a road map the whales travel wherever these forces lead. Unfortunately the magnetic flow will sometimes cross the shoreline and guide the whales along a collision course with the beach.

Biologists realize of course that none of these findings are complete explanations. Some feel that the strandings must have a number of causes not just one.

Next Step In the space above, write freely for 3 to 5 minutes about punctuating writing. Consider what's easy or hard about it, what's important or confusing. Then, double-check your work by reviewing the punctuation rules and examples in *Write Source*.

Punctuation Review 2

Directions **Review rules pages 579–612 in *Write Source*. These rules discuss commas, semicolons, colons, dashes, parentheses, hyphens, question marks, exclamation points, quotation marks, italics, and apostrophes. Then punctuate the following paragraphs correctly.**

Famous celebrities pose for pictures sign autographs and make a lot of money. Going unnoticed however are the other stars the animal actors who work hard to keep these human celebrities in business. These truly great stars are dogs like Timmys Lassie and Marty Cranes Eddie on Frasier .

Lassie is probably the best known television pet. However the dog we all now know as Lassie was not originally cast for the part. He was hired instead as a stunt dog. Pal Lassies real name was a beautiful sable collie and he was trained by Rudd Weatherwax a Hollywood dog trainer.

In one of the early filming sessions for the movie Lassie Come Home Lassie needed to swim across a raging river pull herself out of the water and lie on the bank pretending to be dead. The starring dog who originally played the part of Lassie could not be convinced to step into the water. So Pal the stunt dog was called into action. Pal swam across the raging river even the swirling rapids without any difficulty. He didnt even shake out his coat when he got to the other side he lay down and pretended to be dead. The original starring dog was fired and Pal was hired as the new Lassie.

Eddie the terrier who starred on the TV show Frasier is also a show stealing star. He is the talented dog who sometimes got more laughs than the shows human star Kelsey Grammar. Eddie whose real name is Moose did many comical tricks and made goofy facial expressions that made it seem as though he knew just what would make an audience laugh. He appeared on the covers of these popular magazines Life TV Guide and Entertainment Weekly.

Animal actors are so well trained that we often forget that they cant be taught to act in the same way that humans are taught. Today with movies like Air Bud and Bear animal films are more popular than ever. Thanks to the dedication of their trainers the work of their agents and the talents of these incredible animals we are able to enjoy a whole new generation of animal films and TV shows.

Capitalization 1

Good writers write good sentences. They also check their details and proofread their work to get rid of errors. In this exercise, you will proofread your writing for capitalization errors. The key to capitalizing correctly is remembering to capitalize all proper nouns and proper adjectives. (See 618.1–618.4, 620.5, and 622.2 in *Write Source* to review capitalization rules.)

Examples

Capitalize Historical Events and Proper Nouns:
The 2002 Winter Olympics were in Salt Lake City, Utah.

Capitalize Names and Words Used as Names:
Felix and Aunt Necia went to the games in Sydney, Australia.

Capitalize Titles Used with Names:
For years, President Juan A. Samaranch had been in charge of the games.

Capitalize Particular Sections of the Country:
The West Coast is the perfect place for skiing and sledding competitions.

Directions

Add capital letters to the following sentences as needed. The first sentence has been done for you.

1. The international olympic committee decides where the games will be held.
2. Salt Lake city, utah, was a perfect place for the winter games in 2002.
3. Winter conditions east of Salt lake City are ideal for skiing and skating.
4. The wasatch mountains are east of Salt lake City.
5. During the planning for the games, mayor rocky anderson met with the united states olympic committee.
6. A hare, a coyote, and a bear were the official olympic mascots of the salt lake city games.
7. Their names were swifter, higher, and stronger.

8. Officials from salt lake city hoped that many tourists would come to the games.
9. At our school, we studied the history of utah.
10. mr. markus, our science teacher, visited utah last spring.
11. The olympic flame was first used in the opening ceremonies in the 1936 summer games in berlin.
12. The olympic flag has five rings that represent unity among the continents of africa, the americas, asia, australia, and europe.
13. My uncle was at the competition where Nadia comaneci, a romanian gymnast, earned the first perfect score in olympic gymnastics.
14. The international sports federation decides the rules for gymnastic competitions.
15. World war I forced the cancellation of the 1916 games, planned for berlin, germany.
16. At the 1936 berlin games, african american athlete jesse owens won gold medals in the 100-meter dash, 200-meter dash, and long jump event.
17. Last friday, mayor jackson and five council members attended an Olympic site-selection meeting in new york.
18. The meeting was sponsored by mcDonald's corporation.

Next Step Using the Internet or other sources, research one of the past Olympic Games. Find out who the stars were and write about your findings in a paragraph or two. Share your writing with a classmate. Your classmate should check to see that you've capitalized words correctly.

Capitalization 2

Here's another exercise to help you to capitalize words correctly. Some helpful examples are given below. (See 624.1, 624.2, 626.1, and 626.2 in *Write Source* for more information and rules.

Examples

Capitalize the First Word at the Beginning of a Direct Quotation:
My friend Sasha said, "Well, my favorite Olympic sport is diving."

Capitalize Titles, Days, and Months:
The History of Olympic Games **will be available in our library Friday, February 19.**

Capitalize Organizations and Abbreviations:
The International Olympic Committee is sometimes referred to as the IOC.

Directions **Add capital letters where necessary to the following sentences. The first sentence has been done for you.**

1. The ~~u.s.s.r.~~ U.S.S.R. sent its first ~~o~~ O lympic team to the games in ~~h~~ H elsinki, ~~f~~ F inland.
2. The *encyclopaedia britannica* has a large section on the olympic games.
3. My teacher said that the russians boycotted the games in los angeles because americans boycotted the games in moscow.
4. Felix said, "the winter games were once held in nagano, japan."
5. "I wish that I could have gone," he continued, "but it was too expensive."
6. "Well," I replied, "at least you got to watch the games on tv."
7. The ioc has introduced some new sports to the olympics in the last 10 years.

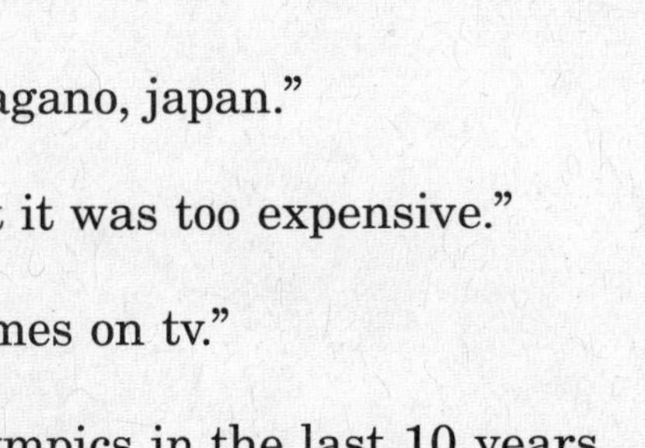

8. "the number of women's sports has certainly increased," said Felicia.
9. my uncle was a speed skater for the dutch team in the 2002 olympics.
10. the winter games were canceled in 1940 and 1944 because of world war II.

11. Chris witty, a u.s. skater, won the 1000-meter speed-skating race in 2002.

12. Is *blade runner* a book about olympic speed skating?

13. *sports illustrated* features many articles about the international stars of the olympic games.

14. After watching the 2002 Winter Olympic Games, my friend Ross said, "those snowboarding events were awesome."

15. The IOC (International Olympic Committee) should not be confused with the iac (International Athletic Conference) or the ibc (International Bowling Congress).

16. Each country that participates in the Olympic Games has a National Olympic Committee (noc) that helps select athletes for its teams.

17. The official Web site of the ioc is called the olympic movement, and it gives information about past, present, and future Olympic Games.

18. I remember my English teacher, mr. Oden, saying, "my favorite sports poem is 'to an Athlete Dying Young' by A. E. Housman."

Next Step Write an imaginary conversation between you and your favorite Olympic or sports champion. Be sure to describe her or him first so that we will know more about the star. Share your writing with a classmate and ask her or him to correct any capitalization errors.

Abbreviations and Numbers

Using abbreviations is convenient, but if you overuse them or use them incorrectly, they can make your writing confusing.

Using numbers can be a bit tricky. The big question is whether you should write numbers out or use figures. The type of writing often determines your choice. In technical, scientific, and business writing, figures are often used. In general writing, however, numbers are more often spelled out. (For more information about numbers and abbreviations, see pages 634, 636, 638, and 640 in *Write Source.*)

Examples

Abbreviations:

Mr. and Mrs. James Wilkins, Jr. are returning from their trip to Ethiopia. (Acceptable)

They came home to the U.S. on Thurs., but they will return to Africa in Dec. (Unacceptable: Do not abbreviate the names of states, countries, days, or months in formal writing.)

Numerals Only:

Please read pages 345–362 in chapter 3 for tomorrow.

Numerals in Compound Modifiers:

I asked for three 13-year-old volunteers.

Correct any abbreviation or number error by drawing a line through the error and writing the correct form above it. Do not change any abbreviation or number that is used correctly. The first sentence has been done for you.

1. ~~12~~ *Twelve* of Hugo's best friends came to visit him.
2. On May six, Hugo and his friends celebrated his 10th birthday.
3. Last year, when Hugo turned nine, his parents bought him a new bike.
4. His father is a prof. who works for nasa.

5. His mother is an m.d. who specializes in ER medicine.
6. Now that he is going to be ten, Hugo is hoping to get 3 presents for his birthday.
7. Someday Hugo would like to work for the cia or fbi, so he wants a spy kit.
8. He would also like 2 250-piece sets of building blocks.
9. The gift he really hopes to receive is an IBM pc.
10. Hugo might have to wait another year for his pc.
11. His pal Joey gave Hugo a geode from Tenn., and his friend Jason gave him a wooden box from Ark.
12. But the strangest gift Hugo received came from his dad's friend Doctor Burns, PHD, a N.A.S.A. rocket scientist.
13. Dr. Burns gave Hugo a twelve-ounce moon rock brought back on *Apollo 17,* which landed on the moon Dec. 11, 1972.
14. Joey hung around, and he and Hugo watched W.W.F. wrestling on the WB network and saw about 1 million commercials.
15. Joey's dad picked him up and drove down Highway thirty-six back to their home.
16. Hugo had a great birthday, but his mom and dad were exhausted from having to deal with 13 10-year-old boys from 10:30 AM to 7:00 PM.

Next Step Write a paragraph about the best birthday present you ever received. Share the paragraph with your classmates and have them check for correct use of abbreviations and numbers.

Capitalization and Abbreviations Review

Attention to detail means different things to different people. To a writer it means carefully reviewing a final draft to make sure that every *i* is dotted, every *t* is crossed, and every capital letter is in place. (See pages 618–626, 634, and 636 in *Write Source* for more information on capitalization and abbreviations.)

Directions **Put a line through any word or letter below that is capitalized or abbreviated incorrectly. Correct each error and add punctuation where needed.**

1. home of mrs goodwrench

2. The Mayor is going to speak Tues.

3. Did you call me, uncle Jim?

4. Go East until you come to the library.

5. Isn't your Mother from the East?

6. This humid august weather is unbearable.

7. I heard mom calling for you, Dad.

8. I've always liked History Courses. Are you taking history 201 next Fall?

9. Mr. Kipp let me read there's a bat in bunk five.

10. Castles were quite common in the Middle ages.

11. Are you going to take that job out west?

12. No, I am going to take the job down South.

13. the Battle of Bunker Hill

14. She shouted, "don't touch the stove!"

15. Navajo pottery, Dutch pastry, Chinese muslin

16. Have you read "by the waters of babylon"?

17. The Chicago Trib. is a fine daily newspaper.

18. George W. Bush was once the governor of TX.

19. "make room," barked the mover. "This piano is heavy."

20. "jerome," yelled coach rogers, "stay back on defense!"

21. They'll put people on the Planet Mars.

22. lakes Michigan and Superior

23. Colorado river

24. the bailey middle school science club will sell refreshments.

25. Bob Madsen, m.d.

26. Mr Jackson, mark's father, joined the staff at Trinity hospital.

27. Kellogg's crispix cereal

28. the first amendment to the constitution of the U S A

29. He's busy with his American History 212 assignment.

30. Hawaii is in the Pacific ocean.

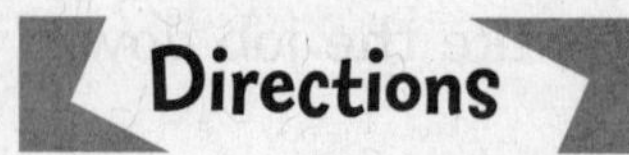

Supply the necessary capital letters in the following narrative. (There are 49 capital letters needed.)

america's best-loved radio program, *a prairie home companion,* left the air on june 13, 1987, at the height of its popularity. broadcast from the world theater in st. paul, minnesota, the show charmed millions of listeners. host garrison keillor took his audience into the heart and soul of an imaginary town in minnesota called lake wobegon—also known by the following title: "the town that time forgot and the decades could not improve." who could ever forget father emil, our lady of perpetual responsibility, the sidetrack tap, bertha's kitty boutique, powdermilk biscuits, ralph's pretty good grocery, and "the statue of the unknown norwegian"? After several years, the show returned to the airwaves due to popular demand.

Capitalization Mixed Review

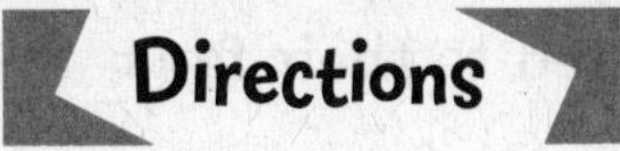

Carefully read the following essay and add capital letters wherever necessary. (For capitalization rules, see pages 618–626 in *Write Source*.)

Baseball legends like babe ruth, hank aaron, roger maris, mark McGwire, and sammy sosa have helped make baseball an all-american pastime. for years fans have crowded into stadiums around the country to witness these home-run hitters at their best.

one of the most gifted and popular players of all time was babe ruth. babe's real name was george herman ruth, and he was born in baltimore, maryland. babe ruth pitched for the boston red sox, played outfield for the new york yankees, and even coached for the brooklyn dodgers. though ruth was very talented in all these areas, the thing he is most remembered for is his home-run hitting. his record of 60 home runs in one season was unchallenged until 1962 when roger maris, another american league player, broke the record with 61 home runs in one season. babe ruth was elected to the baseball hall of fame in 1936.

today, records continue to be broken by modern baseball legends such as mark mcgwire and sammy sosa. these two players both broke maris's record in september 1998. mcgwire, who was born in pomona, california, on october 1, 1963, plays first base for the st. louis cardinals. he ended his 1998 season with a new record of 70 home runs, while sosa finished the season with 66 home runs. mcgwire said in an interview with the *st. louis dispatch,* "this is a season I will never, ever forget, and I hope everybody in baseball never forgets." baseball fans won't soon forget these talented players. not only are they power hitters, but they have also demonstrated to their fans what it means to play with dignity, class, and humility.

although mcgwire hit more home runs than sosa, sosa was voted the 1998 national league most valuable player by the baseball writers association of america. at wrigley field, sosa said, "winning the mvp is not for me; it's for the people of the city of chicago." besides his 66 homers, sosa led the major leagues with 158 rbi's and took the cubs to the national league play-offs.

sosa is from san pedro de macoris in the dominican republic. after the 1998 baseball season, sosa helped the victims of hurricane george. he raised money to buy food for people in the dominican republic and other caribbean countries. sosa also asked the japanese government to send 1,000 prefab houses to the dominican republic.

people in the united states also benefited from this historic home-run derby. seven of sosa and mcgwire's home-run balls were auctioned off. the money from sosa's home-run ball 61 went to the sammy sosa foundation, an organization that helps kids. half the money paid for big mac's number 70 home-run ball also went to charity.

Spelling and Plurals

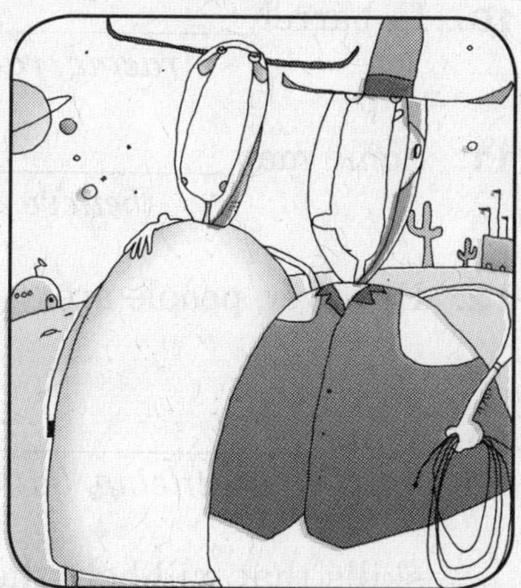

Developing spelling skills takes time and patience. Using your spell checker and a dictionary can help. (See pages 630, 632, and 642 in *Write Source* to review rules about spelling correctly. Also use the guide on pages 645–651.)

Directions **Complete the following sentences by writing the correctly spelled word in parentheses on the line provided. The first sentence has been done for you.**

1. At ___*rodeos*___, cowboys show their skills at ___*handling*___ cattle.
   (*rodeos, rodeoes*) (*handleing, handling*)

2. At these competitions, ____________________ skills are important.
   (*rideing, riding*)

3. Steer ____________________ is a popular event for competitors.
   (*wrestleing, wrestling*)

4. ____________________ is another name for this event.
   (*Bulldogging, Bulldoging*)

5. In this event, the cowboy tries ____________________ the horns of the steer
   (*grabbing, grabing*)
   to twist the head of the animal to one side.

6. The steer loses its balance, ____________________ it to fall to the ground.
   (*forcing, forceing*)

7. Calf ____________________ is another important skill for ranchers and cowboys.
   (*ropeing, roping*)

8. The cowboy ____________________ the calf with a ____________________ rope.
   (*lassoes, lassos*) (*looped, loopped*)

9. The cowboy then ____________________ together three of the calf's ____________________.
   (*ties, tys*) (*feet, feets*)

10. In barrel ________________, competitors ride horses around barrels.
(*racing, raceing*)

11. Some may ________________ rodeos are dangerous for the animals.
(*believe, beleive*)

12. However, people are ________________ not to hurt the animals.
(*careful, carful*)

13. While ________________ these animals, the cowboys are practicing
(*battleing, battling*)

skills that will help them in ________________ their livestock.
(*raiseing, raising*)

14. My family and ________________ are ________________ to helping
(*freinds, friends*) (*committed, commited*)

________________ understand the sport.
(*children, childrens*)

15. In junior rodeos, kids rope goats instead of ________________, but
(*calves, calfs*)

________________ of those animals is easy to rope.
(*niether, neither*)

16. Rodeo clowns throw ________________ of confetti to distract angry bulls.
(*handfuls, handsful*)

17. At the ________________ of their act, some clowns play ________________.
(*beginning, begining*) (*banjoes, banjos*)

18. Rodeo cowboys compete by riding ________________, bulls, and broncos.
(*steers, steeres*)

19. Professional rodeo cowboys buy ________________ hats and boots at the many
(*their, thier*)

Cowboy Country Stores located in the western United States.

Next Step Write a paragraph about an interesting sports event. Share the paragraph with a classmate. Ask the classmate to check your writing for correct spelling and use of plurals.

Using the Right Word 1

It's important to use the right word whenever you are going to share your thoughts in a formal or semi-formal situation. Whenever you have a usage question, refer to "Using the Right Word," pages 652–658 in *Write Source*.

Examples

It's nice to have a lot of friends.

The charity accepts any kind of donation.
All my books except one are covered.

Banks have a large amount of money.
A number of people waited for tickets.

One small tree grew among the flowers.
Nothing comes between those two friends.

I'll bring my comics to your house.
Take these books to the library.

These fries are altogether too salty.
We were all together at the playground.

Dwight already brushed his teeth.
My room is all ready for fresh paint.

Mom brakes for animals in the road.
Did your ball break my window?

Stand beside me for this picture.
Besides soccer, Drew plays tennis.

The base of this lamp is quite heavy.
Regina plays the bass trombone.

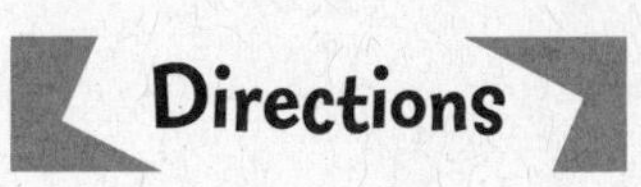

If the underlined word is incorrect, cross out the word and write the correct form above it. Do not change a word that is correct. The first sentence has been done for you.

On a hot summer morning in 1939, the people who lived in tiny Orange City, Iowa, were ~~already~~ *all ready* for the Fourth of July celebration. In the village park, a large cannon lay on a frame among two wooden-spoked wheels. Besides the big gun, three huge balls rested on a square wooden bass. Two uniformed World War I veterans stood on either side of the cannon. A large amount of spectators had gathered around them.

The mayor was just finishing his speech: " . . . and the reason we're altogether in this safe, free, grand country of ours is not simply a result of this being our place of birth. As alot of you older folks remember, when President Wilson told us to take up arms, we all willingly excepted that command. When the call to duty came, we believed that free people cannot remain free when others are trying to brake up their democracy!"

The mayor stabbed his large right hand into the air to emphasize his last point: "So our soldier boys brought nothing accept their guns and bullets over to the other side of the ocean, so they could take back a new lease on freedom to this side of the ocean!"

There were alot of children among the crowd, beside the usual farmers, housewives, and a number of storekeepers. They were all together energized. And now, altogether, they cheered the mayor and the round-shouldered veteran who had all ready lit the fuse on the huge, old cannon.

Next Step Write a short incident report about a recent event that surprised (or frustrated) you. Use five or more of the words you just learned about in this lesson. Circle them. (See pages 150–151 in *Write Source* for writing guidelines and a sample incident report.)

Using the Right Word 2

For examples and explanations, see pages 660–666 in *Write Source*.

Examples

I hope I never see a real prison cell.
Tamika will sell **candy at the game.**

The tree creaks **when the wind blows.**
D. J. likes to go fishing in the creek.

Hunter is such a good **dog.**
Nadine acted well **in the school play.**

A spicy sauce complements **the potatoes.**
Ms. Rau compliments **students on their work.**

This pet store has fewer **birds than that one.**
Dad has less **hair now than when he was 20.**

We heard **the bell ringing miles away.**
A herd **of mountain goats crossed the road.**

If the underlined word is incorrect, cross out the word and write the correct form above it. Do not change a word that is correct. The first sentence has been done for you.

1. Monique ~~herd~~ *heard* a ~~creek~~ *creak* every time she stepped on a certain spot on the floor.
2. The longer you stay in bed after sunrise, the less things you'll accomplish that day.
3. You'll get along good with others if you give compliments when they are deserved.
4. Have you even seen a herd of cattle grazing near a creak in a farm field?
5. I might try to cell my stamp collection.
6. Wow, Rita, that shade of blue really compliments your hair and skin.
7. This is a well plant for desert climates since it requires fewer water than most others.
8. The sell of a honeycomb has six sides.
9. I herd a little creek from the cricket out on our back porch.

Using the Right Word 3

For examples and explanations, see pages 668–676 in *Write Source*.

Examples

A contractor will lay the carpet tomorrow.
Rudy will lie in the hammock for hours.

I need two lead pencils for the test.
Seiko led the horse to the barn.

John Lennon said, "Give peace a chance."
Cut me a piece of that pie.

It looks like it's going to storm.
This book is missing some of its pages.

Don't leave the milk on the counter.
Mom will not let me pierce my navel.

My principal goal is to go to college.
I follow the principle of "honesty always."

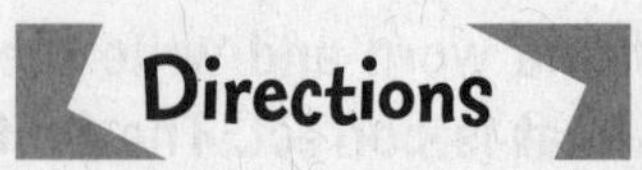

Correct any errors by drawing a line through the word and writing the correct form above it. Do not change any word that is correct. The first sentence has been done for you.

1. Based on the ~~principals~~ *principles* of science, I have been ~~lead~~ *led* to believe that clean energy is in our future.
2. If LaTanya and Jawann would just let each other alone, there would be piece in the house!
3. Its rare for my cat to lay anywhere except the windowsill on a sunny day.
4. "I can see that lead statue is heavy," said Scott. "Please leave me carry it."
5. He said, "Go ahead and lie it right here on the floor for a minute."
6. The principle reason Corentine's chameleon lost a peace of it's tail was that someone had stepped on it.
7. There are two principals that I try to live out—being dependable and respectful.

Sentence Activities

The activities in this section cover three important areas: (1) the basic parts of sentences, (2) common sentence errors, and (3) ways to add variety to sentences. Most activities include a main practice part in which you review, combine, or analyze different sentences. In addition, the **Next Step** activities give you follow-up practice with certain skills.

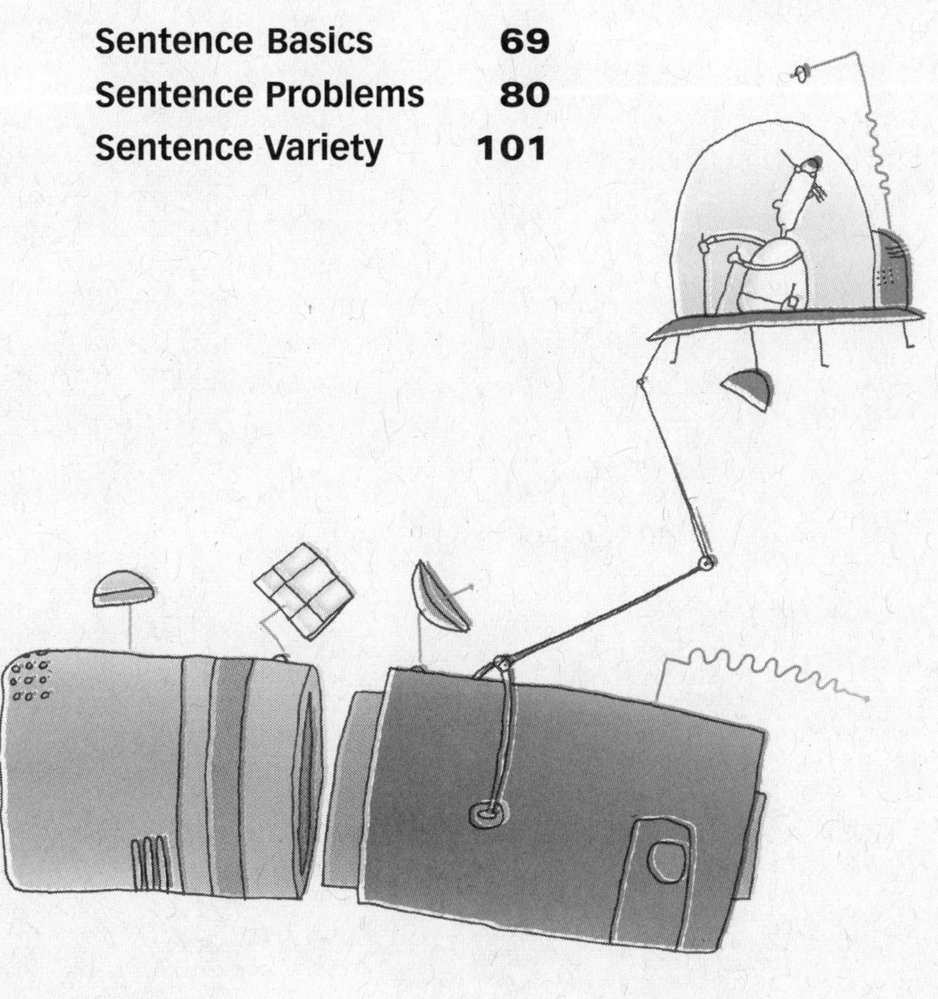

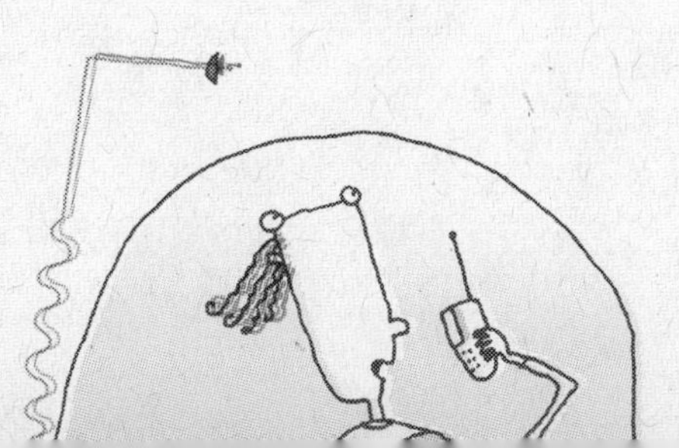

Subjects and Predicates 1

Careful writers write clear and complete sentences. A sentence consists of two parts: the subject and the predicate. The **subject** is the part that is doing something or about which something is being said. The **predicate** is the part that says something about the subject. In a sentence, the subject and predicate fit together to form a complete thought. (See 690.2, 692.2, and 694.1 in *Write Source* to examine subjects and predicates in more detail.)

Examples

Simple Subject:

Marjorie owns a robot that carries her books for her.
(The simple subject is who or what the sentence is about.)

Simple Predicate:

Felicia's robot will obey all her commands.
(The predicate—or verb—tells something about the subject. *Remember:* helping verbs like "will" are often part of the simple predicate.)

Understood Subject:

Think about what a robot could do in your home. (understood subject: You)
(When the sentence is a command or a request, the subject is usually not stated. The person to whom the command is directed—"You"—is the subject of the sentence.)

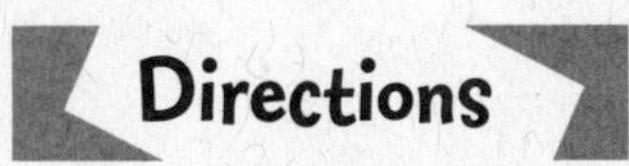

In the following sentences, underline the simple subject once and the simple predicate twice. The first sentence has been done for you.

1. Robots work in homes, businesses, and schools.
2. In medical laboratories, robots handle hazardous materials.
3. At the General Motors Corporation, robots work on assembly lines performing tasks like welding and painting.
4. Most boring or dangerous tasks are done by GMC's robots.

5. Other companies use specially designed robots for tasks that require precision.

6. Robots explore sunken ships, distant planets, and active volcanoes.

7. Miguel's toy soldier is really a small robot.

8. Think of all the robot-like toys you own. (*You*)

9. Jeremiah dreams of owning his own robot someday.

10. Elena wishes for a robot to do her math homework for her.

11. I want robots for mowing my lawn, delivering my newspapers, and cleaning my room.

12. Maybe my teacher will be replaced by a computerized robot.

13. Imagine what the world would be like with thousands of robots. (*You*)

14. One of the stars of *The Red Planet* was Robby the Robot.

15. Have you ever seen a robot at work?

16. Our family's robot could get me a glass of milk.

17. Most robots in films and TV shows are not very realistic.

18. Can you name your favorite robot?

Next Step Imagine having your own robot. Write a paragraph describing what your personal robot would be like. Then draw an illustration to accompany your paragraph. Share the illustration and the paragraph with a classmate. Have your classmate check your writing for complete sentences.

Subjects and Predicates 2

There are simple subjects and simple predicates. But what about all those other words in the sentence? The words that describe the subject or predicate are called *modifiers.* Modifiers change or add to the meaning of the subject or predicate. Together, the simple subject plus its modifiers make the **complete subject,** and the simple predicate plus its modifiers make the **complete predicate.** (See 690.3 and 692.3 in *Write Source* for more information.)

Examples

Complete Subject:

The large, umbrella-shaped parachute saved the life of the inexperienced pilot.

(The complete subject is the simple subject—"parachute"—plus all its modifiers.)

Complete Predicate:

The large, umbrella-shaped parachute saved the life of the inexperienced pilot.

(The complete predicate is the simple predicate—"saved"—plus all its modifiers.)

In the following sentences, divide the complete subject and the complete predicate with a slash (/). Then, underline the simple subject once and the simple predicate twice. The first sentence has been done for you.

1. French aeronaut Jean Pierre Blanchard/dropped a dog in the first parachute "jump" in 1785.
2. Blanchard successfully made the first human parachute drop in 1793.
3. Parachutes are now required for all balloonists and pilots.
4. The large silk or nylon parachute canopy has a small vent hole in its center that expands to lessen the shock when the parachute opens.

5. The 24-foot, multipaneled parachute is pulled from the jumper's backpack by a smaller parachute.

6. Parachutes have been used during wars to drop troops, tanks, and equipment behind enemy lines.

7. Sport parachuting, also known as skydiving, became popular in the 1970s.

8. Steerable parachutes that allow safer landings have made the sport even more popular today.

9. Parachutists compete in skydiving competitions by doing a series of aerobatic maneuvers before reaching parachute-opening altitude.

10. Teams of free-falling skydivers compete by forming as many geometric patterns as possible before opening their chutes.

11. (You) Consider the risk of skydiving before taking the plunge.

12. Steerable parachutes are quite different from hang gliders.

13. In 1972, a Yugoslavian flight attendant survived a fall from 33,370 feet without a parachute.

14. The record for the longest fall with a parachute is 40 minutes.

Next Step Skydiving is a sport that requires skill and daring. Write a paragraph explaining why you would or would not want to be a skydiver. Share the paragraph with a classmate. Be sure to write in complete sentences.

Compound Subjects and Predicates

Combining short, related sentences into longer sentences is valuable practice for improving your writing style. Writers can combine short sentences using coordinating conjunctions. This can result in a sentence with either a **compound subject** (two or more simple subjects) or a **compound predicate** (two or more simple predicates) or both. (For more information about compound subjects and compound predicates, see 690.4 and 692.6 in *Write Source.*)

Examples

Compound Subject:
Earl and Kultida Woods are the proud parents of golf champion Tiger Woods.

Compound Predicate:
Tiger Woods putted against Bob Hope at age two and was featured in *Golf Digest* at age five.

Compound Subject and Compound Predicate:
Tiger and his father play golf and support charities.

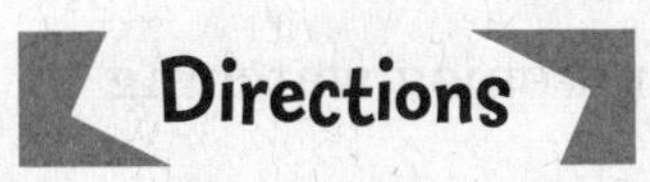

In the following sentences, underline the subject with one line and the predicate with two lines. Remember that some sentences have only a compound subject, some have only a compound predicate, and some have both. The first one has been done for you.

1. Tiger Woods became a professional golfer and won two PGA Tour victories in 1996.

2. Keenan and Angelica watched Tiger play in the tournament and got his autograph at the ninth hole.

3. Tiger and his family traveled to the Asian Honda Classic Golf Tournament in Thailand.

4. In just one year, Tiger won several tournaments, made a lot of money, and earned the respect of other professional golfers.

5. Tiger's father and mother taught him that all people deserve the chance to live out their dreams.

6. Tiger and his father created and actively support a foundation that gives minorities opportunities to play golf.

7. Many awards, trophies, and medals decorate Tiger's home.

8. In their spare time, Tiger and his friends play basketball and go fishing.

9. Mary Lou Retton, the gymnast, and Tiger Woods are the two youngest athletes to be named "Sportsperson of the Year" by *Sports Illustrated.*

10. Young men and women admire Tiger for both his skill and his modesty.

11. Can you or your friend think of a more exciting golfer than Tiger?

12. Over the past few years, Tiger has played well and created a renewed interest in golf.

13. Young people and old people alike admire Tiger's talent and enjoy watching him play.

14. Because of his popularity, many companies and nonprofit organizations have asked Tiger to be a spokesperson for them.

Next Step Using the Internet or other sources, research a sports or entertainment figure. Write a paragraph or two about your findings using some compound subjects and compound predicates. Share your writing with a classmate and ask him or her to check for complete sentences and proper use of compound subjects and predicates.

Clauses

Clauses, like phrases, are word groups that add information to a sentence. Unlike phrases, clauses always have a subject and a predicate. Clauses that form a complete thought are called **independent clauses,** and clauses that do not form a complete thought are called **dependent** or **subordinate clauses.** (*Write Source* gives more information about clauses on page 698.)

Examples

Dependent Clause:

Even though she was at the peak of her career, **Florence Griffith-Joyner retired from running in 1989.**

Independent Clause:

Florence Griffith-Joyner retired from running in 1989 **even though she was at the peak of her career.**

Florence Griffith-Joyner was a fantastic runner, **and** she won many Olympic medals.

(Two independent clauses are separated by a comma and a coordinating conjunction or by a semicolon.)

In each of the following sentences, identify the italicized clause. Write "I" for independent or "D" for dependent. The first sentence has been done for you.

___I___ **1.** Though she grew up in a poor section of South Los Angeles, *Griffith-Joyner overcame poverty to become a world-class runner.*

______ **2.** *Florence Griffith-Joyner was known by the nickname "FloJo,"* but sports fans also knew her as the fastest woman in the world.

______ **3.** *After she won the silver medal in the 200-meter dash in the 1984 Olympics,* Griffith-Joyner retired from her running career.

______ **4.** She began competing again in 1987, and *she earned second place at the World Championship Games in Rome.*

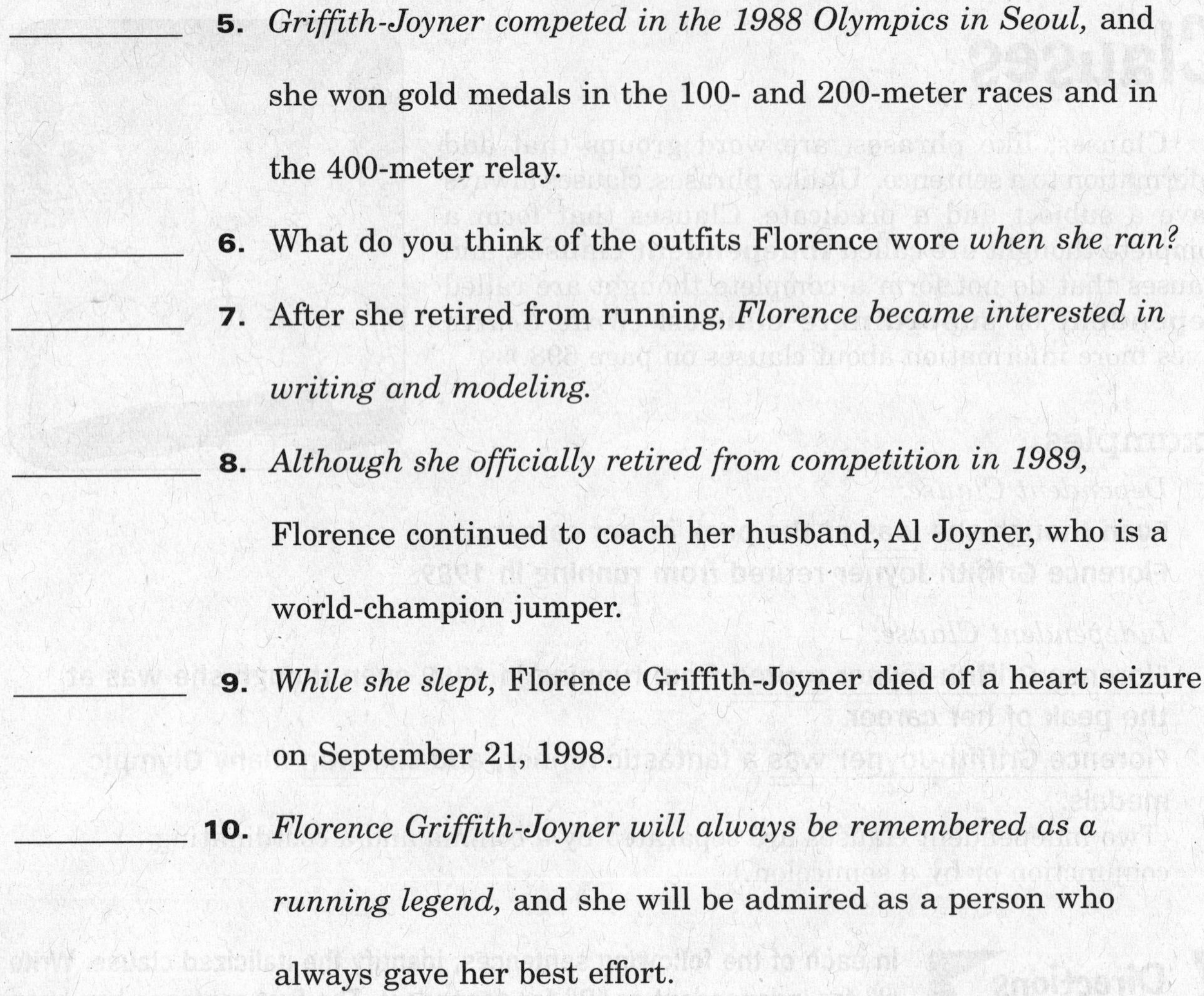

_______ **5.** *Griffith-Joyner competed in the 1988 Olympics in Seoul,* and she won gold medals in the 100- and 200-meter races and in the 400-meter relay.

_______ **6.** What do you think of the outfits Florence wore *when she ran?*

_______ **7.** After she retired from running, *Florence became interested in writing and modeling.*

_______ **8.** *Although she officially retired from competition in 1989,* Florence continued to coach her husband, Al Joyner, who is a world-champion jumper.

_______ **9.** *While she slept,* Florence Griffith-Joyner died of a heart seizure on September 21, 1998.

_______ **10.** *Florence Griffith-Joyner will always be remembered as a running legend,* and she will be admired as a person who always gave her best effort.

Next Step Do some research using the Internet or another source to discover more about Joyner. Try to write five sentences using dependent and independent clauses. Share your writing with a classmate and check each other's work for correct use of clauses.

Phrases

A phrase is a group of words that lacks a subject, a predicate, or both. In many cases, a phrase works as a modifier (describes something) in a sentence. Most phrases are named for the function they serve in a sentence (noun phrase, adverb phrase, verb phrase). Study the examples below and the ones on page 700 in *Write Source*.

Examples

Noun Phrase: **Our summer trip** (This phrase acts as a noun.)

Prepositional Phrase: **to Florida** (This phrase modifies the subject "trip.")

Verb Phrase: **was spent** (This phrase acts as a verb.)

Adverb Phrase: **very excitedly** (This phrase modifies the verb "was spent.")

Verbal Phrase: **viewing the many sights** (This phrase modifies "was spent.")

Identify the underlined phrase in each sentence below. The first sentence has been done for you.

adverb phrase **1.** Early this morning, the Phillips family left for the airport.

________ **2.** They waited at the busy airport to catch their flight to Orlando, Florida.

________ **3.** During their wait, they talked very excitedly about visiting the special attractions at the amusement park.

________ **4.** Mikah was going to see all the exhibits, which feature the cultures of 11 different countries.

________ **5.** People of every age enjoy this exciting and educational experience.

_______________ **6.** Having a tight budget, Mikah and Ruby's parents were determined not to spend too much money.

_______________ **7.** With a tour package, they were able to save money on entrance passes to the amusement park.

_______________ **8.** Ruby has been dreaming about this vacation for years.

_______________ **9.** The Phillips's vacation lasted for five days.

Directions **Write 5 sentences below about a trip you took (or would like to take). Use a different type of phrase in each sentence. Underline the phrases.**

1. ____

____

____

2. ____

____

____

3. ____

____

____

4. ____

____

____

5. ____

____

____

Transitions

All writing should read smoothly and move clearly (logically) from one point to the next. Transitional or linking words like *also, finally,* and *later* and the repetition of key words or phrases can help make your writing smooth reading and clear. (See pages 572–573 in *Write Source* for a list of many different linking words.)

Many of the linking words have been taken out of the paragraph below. Read the paragraph and fill in each blank with a linking word or expression that helps the paragraph flow smoothly from one point to the next. Share your results.

When I was younger, I was always begging my parents to let me cook something by myself. ____________________, my father said he'd teach me how to fry an egg. What a mess! ________________, we got out all the dishes and utensils we needed—frying pan, pot holder, spatula, cup, plate, and fork. ________________, we got the eggs and margarine from the refrigerator. ________________ accidentally smashing one egg on the floor and letting another roll into the sink, I finally managed to crack an egg into the cup and throw the shell into the garbage. ____________, I heated a little margarine in the frying pan and slowly poured the egg from the cup into the pan. Flipping the egg over when it was done on one side was the hardest part. Melted margarine sure splatters. ______________, when it was time to lift my breakfast out of the pan, I discovered how slippery fried eggs are. ________________ a few tries, I did manage to slide my over-easy egg onto the plate, but there was nothing easy about it. ________________, it was time to eat. ________________ cooking was more work than I had expected, that egg tasted great!

Sentence Fragments

A sentence is more than a random collection of words and phrases, just as an airplane is more than a pile of parts and pieces. (Neither will "fly" with parts missing.) A sentence must contain a subject and a predicate, which are arranged with other words to form a complete thought. A sentence that does not express a complete thought is called a **sentence fragment.** (See pages 503 and 504 in *Write Source* for more information about fragments.)

Examples

Sentence Fragment:	*Complete Sentence:*
Are slender and furry.	**Otters are slender and furry.**
(A subject is missing.)	(A subject has been added.)
Sentence Fragment:	*Complete Sentence:*
The furry otter.	**The furry otter is related to the weasel.**
(A predicate is missing.)	(A predicate has been added.)

Identify the following groups of words with an "S" for each sentence or an "F" for each fragment. The first one has been done for you.

__F__ **1.** The otter's oily fur, which forms a waterproof coat.

__S__ **2.** River otters, once common in North America, are rarely seen.

__F__ **3.** Are afraid of humans.

__S__ **4.** Chattering noisily, they take turns sliding down snowy or muddy banks and belly flopping into the water.

__F → S__ **5.** Webbed toes and strong tails make otters excellent swimmers.

__S → F__ **6.** Paddling with their feet and using their strong tails to steer.

__F__ **7.** Prized for their rich fur like their relative the mink.

__F → S__ **8.** In the 1880s, otters were trapped heavily and began disappearing.

__F__ **9.** Are now a protected species with many programs to help them.

Comma Splices and Run-Ons 1

A **comma splice** occurs when you incorrectly connect two simple sentences with a comma instead of a period, semicolon, or connecting word.

A **run-on sentence** occurs when you incorrectly join two simple sentences without using any punctuation. (A period, a semicolon, or a comma and a coordinating conjunction are ways of correcting run-ons.) Both comma splices and run-on sentences can be avoided if you carefully review each of your sentences before sharing your writing with your readers. (For more information, see page 506 in *Write Source*.)

Example

Comma Splice:
Bamboo is a giant form of grass, its shoots are a tasty vegetable.

Run-On:
Bamboo is a giant form of grass its shoots are a tasty vegetable.

Corrected Sentences:
Bamboo is a giant form of grass. Its shoots are a tasty vegetable. ***(or)***
Bamboo is a giant form of grass, and its shoots are a tasty vegetable.

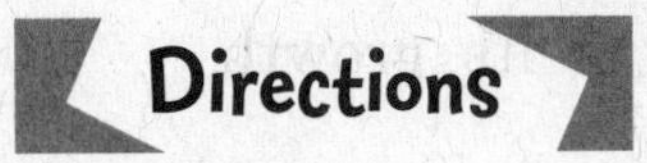

Place a "CS" in front of each comma splice, an "RO" in front of each run-on sentence, and a "C" in front of each correct sentence. Correct each faulty sentence. The first sentence has been done for you.

_CS_ **1.** Bamboo is definitely one of the most interesting plants, *and* it is valued for its beauty and usefulness.

_____ **2.** Bamboo may be one of the world's most useful plants.

_____ **3.** Bamboo grows in huge groves it serves as a natural buffer against floods and erosion.

_____ **4.** In addition, bamboo enriches the soil.

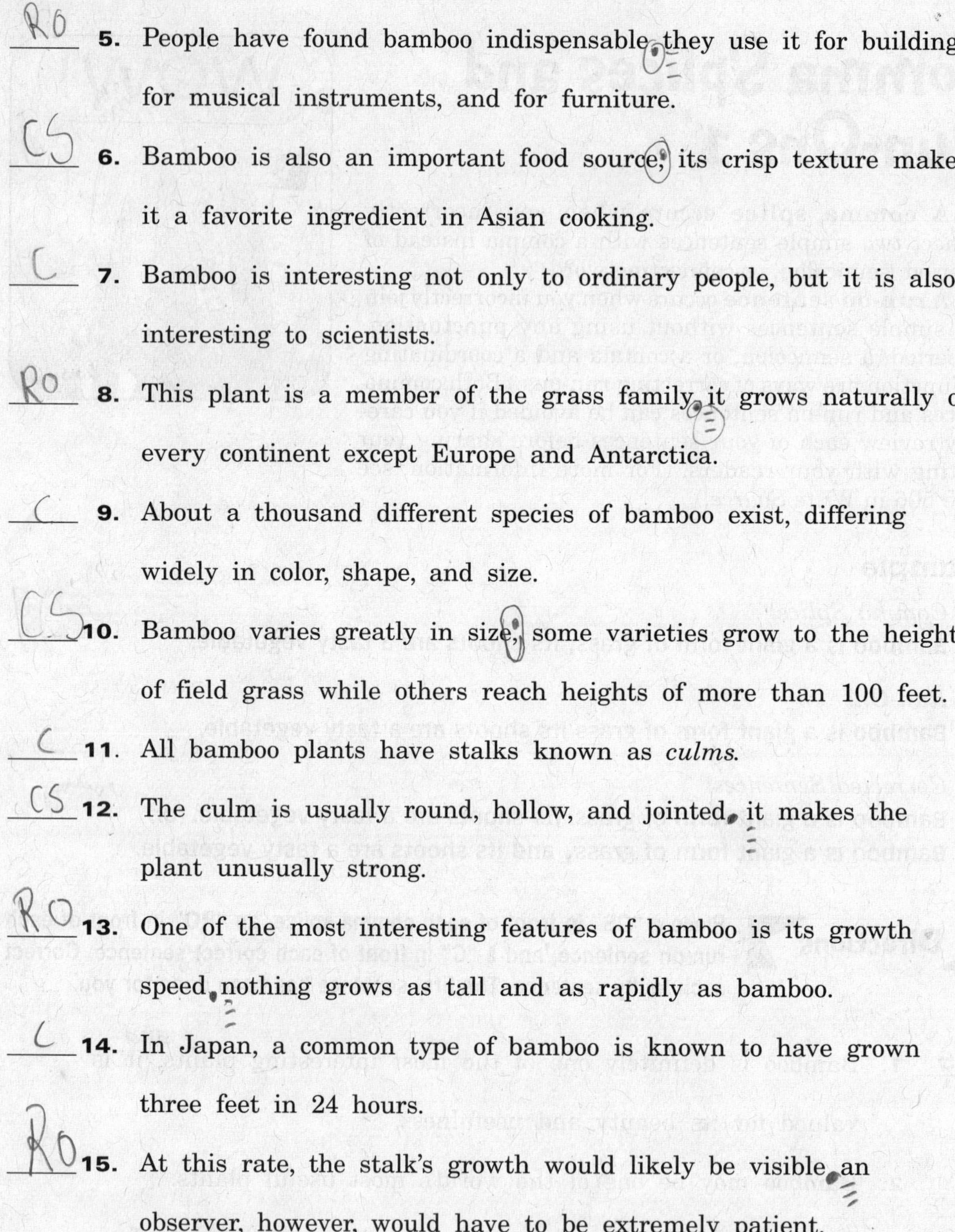

_____ **5.** People have found bamboo indispensable they use it for buildings, for musical instruments, and for furniture.

_____ **6.** Bamboo is also an important food source, its crisp texture makes it a favorite ingredient in Asian cooking.

_____ **7.** Bamboo is interesting not only to ordinary people, but it is also interesting to scientists.

_____ **8.** This plant is a member of the grass family it grows naturally on every continent except Europe and Antarctica.

_____ **9.** About a thousand different species of bamboo exist, differing widely in color, shape, and size.

_____ **10.** Bamboo varies greatly in size, some varieties grow to the height of field grass while others reach heights of more than 100 feet.

_____ **11.** All bamboo plants have stalks known as *culms.*

_____ **12.** The culm is usually round, hollow, and jointed, it makes the plant unusually strong.

_____ **13.** One of the most interesting features of bamboo is its growth speed nothing grows as tall and as rapidly as bamboo.

_____ **14.** In Japan, a common type of bamboo is known to have grown three feet in 24 hours.

_____ **15.** At this rate, the stalk's growth would likely be visible an observer, however, would have to be extremely patient.

Next Step Sometimes it's easier to catch sentence errors in someone else's writing than in your own. (You are, in a sense, too close to your own work.) Exchange a piece of writing in progress with a classmate and check each other's work for comma splices and run-on sentences.

Comma Splices and Run-Ons 2

Combining several related thoughts into the same sentence can be a good thing. You just need to avoid two pitfalls: **run-on sentences** and **comma splices.** Enthusiastic or fast writers often make these errors in their early drafts, but careful editing can correct these problems. Experiment with different punctuation—periods, semicolons—and different connecting, words —*and, but, nor, or, yet, for*—to get the effect you want. (See page 506 in *Write Source* for more information.)

Examples

Incorrect:
He swung at the ball, he missed it.

Correct:
He swung at the ball; he missed it.
He swung at the ball, but he missed it.
He swung at the ball. He missed it.

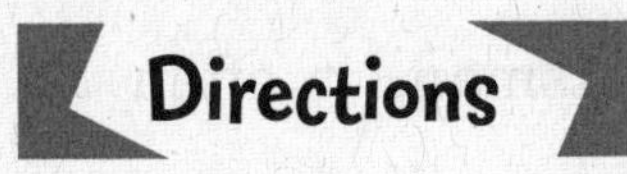

Directions **In the groups of words below, place a "CS" before each comma splice and an "RO" before each run-on sentence. Then correct each error. If a sentence is correct, place a "C" before the sentence. The first one has been done for you.**

CS **1.** Some people are afraid of spiders, other people think they are a sign of good luck.

____ **2.** Most spiders are strange-looking creatures most aren't harmful to people.

____ **3.** Spiders are often used in monster films these spiders are huge.

____ **4.** Spiders have eight eyes, they have eight legs, too.

____ **5.** Spiders have fangs most have poisonous fangs to paralyze their prey.

_____ **6.** Not every spider spins webs, but each one has spinnerets, which allows it to spin fine silk threads.

_____ **7.** Silk is used by different types of spiders for different things it can be used for webs and for wrapping victims.

_____ **8.** Baby spiders of some species (called "parachuters") spin long thin threads and are carried away by the wind, scattering over a wide area.

_____ **9.** The trap-door spider actually makes a hinged door it digs a hole in the ground and closes the door over the hole.

_____ **10.** The California trap-door spider is so strong that it can resist a force 38 times its weight.

_____ **11.** Black widow spiders can actually be deadly, their bites can cause illness and sometimes even death to humans.

_____ **12.** The most venomous spider is the Brazilian huntsman, it often hides in people's shoes.

_____ **13.** The largest spider ever found had a leg span of 11 inches the smallest spider was the size of a period on this page.

_____ **14.** Why do some spiders buzz and others purr?

Next Step How do you feel about spiders? Write a paragraph describing your personal feelings about spiders. Use your own paper.

Sentence Problems Review 1

Good sentences are essential to good writing. In order to write good sentences, you need to avoid some basic sentence errors. Three of the more common sentence errors are **run-on sentences, comma splices,** and **sentence fragments.** (See *Write Source* pages 503–504 and 506 to review these errors, or look back to specific exercises you have already completed on each type of error.)

Place an "RO" in front of each run-on sentence that follows. Place a "CS" in front of each comma splice and an "F" before each sentence fragment. Then fix each error. The first one has been done for you.

RO **1.** Last night, Sam and I biked to the arena to see Garbage in concert; it was a very interesting ride.

_____ **2.** Our route through downtown traffic.

_____ **3.** Biking soon became tricky, the roads were jammed with traffic heading for the concert.

_____ **4.** Impatient drivers blowing their car horns.

_____ **5.** Sam was really nervous about all the traffic, he wasn't used to bumper-to-bumper cars.

_____ **6.** More like New York City than Madison, Wisconsin.

_____ **7.** We were riding in the bike lane, cars kept edging over toward us.

_____ **8.** We finally made it to the arena Sam confessed he had been worried we wouldn't make it.

_____ **9.** Sitting so far back that the musicians looked like ants.

_____ **10.** The sound was great, though we probably heard better than the people in the front row.

Sentence Problems Review 2

Directions **Put an "RO" in front of any run-on sentences that follow, a "CS" in front of any comma splices, and an "F" in front of any fragments. Then fix each error. (Refer to pages 503–504 and 506 in *Write Source* for explanations and examples.)**

_______ **1.** My dad is a long-time member of our town's volunteer fire department, he also belongs to our local rescue squad.

_______ **2.** Always getting called to a fire or an accident right in the middle of supper or when his favorite football team is playing on television.

_______ **3.** One night he rescued two kittens from a burning barn and brought them home we named the kittens Sparky and Soot.

_______ **4.** Still have both kittens 10 years later.

_______ **5.** The kittens are all grown up now, they have become regular members of our family.

_______ **6.** I'll never forget the night we got Sparky and Soot they were cold and smelled like smoke.

_______ **7.** Tiny heads poking out of the pockets of my dad's big rubber coat.

_______ **8.** I thought they were toys, I heard them meow.

_______ **9.** For a child, there many things cuter than baby kittens?

_______ **10.** My sister and I loved the kittens we took them up in our tree house and everywhere we went.

Rambling Sentences

Just as you should correct any fragments, run-ons, or comma splices in your writing, you should also be careful not to use too many *and*'s or *but*'s. The result could be a series of rambling sentences. (See page 507 in *Write Source* for more information.)

Directions **In the following passage (a rewritten scene from *The Adventures of Tom Sawyer* by Mark Twain), look for sentences that ramble on and on. Fix them by taking out some (but not all) of the *and*'s, *but*'s, or *so*'s. Also, add punctuation and capitalization as needed.**

Tom typically carried treasures in his pocket, but this particular Sunday, the "pinch bug" (a large black beetle with formidable jaws) was taken out and the beetle helped himself to Tom's finger and was thereby flicked into the church aisle but a poodle, in church with his master, saw the bug, came up to it, and started to play with it and the poodle's chin got too close and the chin was seized, there was a yelp, and the pinch bug went flying farther down the aisle so the poodle moved toward the beetle, became distracted by a fly, forgot about the beetle entirely and sat down on it and with a wild yelp, the dog went streaking up the aisle like a woolly comet. In desperation, the dog jumped on his master's lap and was flung out of a nearby window and people snickered, the sermon ended, and Tom went home quite satisfied except for one thing he didn't mind that the dog had played with his pinch bug but he did not think it right of the dog to carry it off.

Next Step Write a paragraph about a memorable animal experience. Exchange first drafts with a classmate. Check each other's writing for any rambling sentences and checkmark those sentences that need to be rewritten. Return the papers and make corrections as necessary.

Wordiness

In a popular book about writing entitled *Elements of Style*, the authors stress the importance of clear writing. They explain that you write clearly by removing unnecessary words or phrases.

Example

Wordy Sentence:

I kept thinking about all the things I needed to remember to take along for tomorrow's fishing trip—my lures, the rods, the bait.

Clearer Sentence:

I kept thinking about everything I needed for tomorrow's trip—my lures, rods, bait.

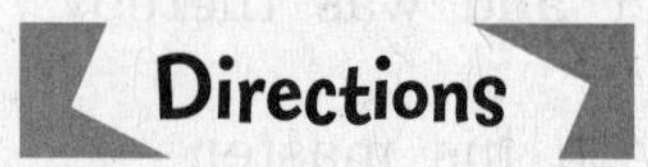

Read the model paragraph and cross out any words that you think are unnecessary. (Some sentences can be corrected in more than one way.)

(1) It was late—time to go to sleep if we wanted to get up ~~early~~ at 4:00 a.m. ~~in the morning~~ for some good fishing. **(2)** But we needed worms and were too excited to sleep which goes without saying. **(3)** We carefully slid the patio door open with great care, trying hard to keep quiet and not make any noise either. **(4)** There was a light fog that seemed to cling to everything it touched. **(5)** Closing the door slowly, we stepped softly onto the patio. **(6)** My friend, he turned on his flashlight so we could see better in the haze. **(7)** We found the worm box on the garage shelf and headed for the flower garden, walking toward it from the garage. **(8)** I flashed my flashlight at the moist ground and spotted a couple of fat night crawlers slipping back into their holes and sliding under the ground to escape. **(9)** My friend grabbed them just in time and dropped them into the box. **(10)** On we went, shining our lights and grabbing worms until we had plenty of bait that would be enough for a morning of fishing. **(11)** My friend and I, we were tired as we put everything away and sneaked back to our room, finally ready to get some rest before our fishing trip.

Next Step Check at least one of your most recent writings and eliminate any unnecessary words you may have included.

Double Negatives and Incorrect Usage

As you talk with your friends, you'll probably hear a lot of *nonstandard language.* What is natural in spoken language can be confusing in written communication.

Though double negatives are common in song lyrics and casual speech, you should avoid them when writing, unless you are quoting someone or creating an informal sentence. (See page 510 in *Write Source* for more information.)

Examples

Incorrect:
We don't need no money.
(Does this mean "We don't need money" or "We need money"?)

Correct:
We don't need any money.
(The meaning—"We don't need money"—is clear.)

Incorrect:
I didn't barely pass the test.
(Does this sentence mean "I did pass"? Or does it mean "I didn't pass"?)

Correct:
I barely passed the test.
(The meaning—"I passed the test"—is clear.)

Note: Do not use *hardly, barely,* or *scarcely* with a negative word; the result is a double negative.

Directions **Write the correct negative for each sentence below. The first one has been done for you.**

1. There ___*is hardly any*___ time to practice before the soccer game.
(isn't hardly no, is hardly any)

2. Chocolate can poison canines, so never to give __________ to your dog.
(any, none)

3. We don't need __________ heroes—just a few true friends.
(no, any)

4. Antarctica doesn't have ______________ of the food plants of other climates.
(none, any)

5. Antarctica's ice contains algae that ______________ bigger than a single cell.
(aren't no, are no)

6. Shrimplike krill, ______________________________ than the single-celled
(scarcely no bigger, scarcely bigger)

plants, eat the algae and become part of the food chain that supports whales, penguins, and seals.

7. I can't think of ________________ better than living on a houseboat.
(nothing, anything)

8. Our parrot doesn't say ______________ words, but he mimics the sounds of
(no, any)

our dishwasher, our telephone, and the family cat!

9. Aaron didn't have ______________ money for a boat, so he made a raft.
(no, any)

10. Scarcely ______________ showed up to audition for the school play.
(nobody, anybody)

11. Later that year, so many people tried out for *West Side Story* that we

____________________________ all cram into the practice gym.
(couldn't hardly, could hardly)

12. Ann didn't want ______________ part of Jake's plan to put sea monkeys in
(no, any)

Miss Han's classroom aquarium.

Next Step Collect several examples of standard and nonstandard language from magazines, TV, and the radio. Jot them down on a sheet of paper. Explain why each example is an appropriate (or inappropriate) piece for its intended audience and purpose.

Misplaced Modifiers

Modifiers are words, phrases, and clauses that describe the simple subject or simple predicate of the sentence. The key to using modifiers effectively is to make sure that you place them as close as possible to the words they modify. Misplacing the modifier makes a sentence confusing and sometimes silly. (See page 505 in *Write Source* to examine misplaced modifiers in more detail.)

Example

Confusing Sentence:
John Glenn returned to space shortly after turning 77 on October 29, 1998.
(It sounds as if John Glenn turned 77 on October 29, 1998.)

Clear Sentence:
Shortly after turning 77, John Glenn returned to space on October 29, 1998.

Directions **Rewrite the following sentences to correct the misplaced modifiers. The first one has been done for you.**

1. John Glenn relaxed on the day before the flight with his family.

   On the day before the flight, John Glenn relaxed with his family.

2. He was eager to begin his second flight into space with all the media in attendance.

   ____

   ____

3. After being away from flight for many years, the new space program was an opportunity that Glenn couldn't resist.

   ____

   ____

4. The space crew spent the morning adjusting their bulky space suits along with John Glenn.

5. Because he's the oldest American astronaut to fly in space, one reporter decided to publish a book about John Glenn and his flight.

6. Many local residents were able to watch the launch of the space shuttle from their own backyards.

7. Wearing bulky space suits, the ground crew helped the astronauts board the shuttle.

8. The president of the United States came to watch the space shuttle lift off with a congressional delegation.

Next Step John Glenn was the first U.S. astronaut to orbit the earth. Using the Internet or other research tools, find out more about him and his career. Then write a paragraph about your findings. Ask a classmate to check your writing for misplaced modifiers.

Subject-Verb Agreement 1

The subject and the verb of a sentence must agree in number. In other words, if the subject is singular, the verb must be singular, too. If the subject is plural, then the verb must be plural. (See pages 508 and 509 in *Write Source* for more information and examples.)

Examples

Compound Subjects:

Annie and her roommate are riding to the concert in our van.

(Compound subjects connected by "and" need a plural verb.)

Neither Annie nor her friends are riding home with us.

(With compound subjects connected by "or" or "nor," the verb must agree with the subject nearest to the verb.)

Collective Noun Subjects:

Camp staff report for duty a week before camp begins.

("Staff" is plural because each member will be coming from a different place.)

This staff is the best group of counselors in Camp Gichagoomie's history.

(The members of the staff are referred to as one group, so the verb is singular.)

Write the correct form of the verb in the sentences below. The first sentence has been done for you.

1. A skunk and its enemy ___*are*___ soon parted.
   (is, are)

2. The crew ____________ in groups of four between 11:30 a.m. and 1:30 p.m.
   (eats, eat)

3. Beans and Barley Restaurant ____________ great veggie burgers.
   (serve, serves)

4. Neither the weather nor the traffic ____________ to blame for the accident.
   (was, were)

5. Either math or pre-algebra __________ a requirement for eighth graders.
(is, are)

6. Congress rarely ________________ its agenda before it adjourns.
(complete, completes)

7. Cotton candy, carnival rides, and fireworks ___________ state fairs fun.
(makes, make)

8. The Cornhuskers and the Jayhawks ___________ bound to meet in the Big
(is, are)

Eight conference play-offs this year.

9. Your mother, father, or legal guardian __________ required to sign your
(is, are)

permission slip.

10. The Summerfest crowd __________ disbanding when the rain started.
(was, were)

11. Each twin __________ challenges as one or the other makes new friends.
(faces, face)

12. Neither the faculty nor the students __________ happy with the old gym.
(was, were)

13. The committee __________ recommended improvements for school lunches.
(has, have)

14. Buses and bicycles __________ the credit for reducing air pollution.
(shares, share)

15. The little pig who built his house of bricks claimed that work and play

____________ mix!
(doesn't, don't)

Next Step As a class, talk about examples of subject-verb agreement that seem tricky or confusing. Then write a tricky sentence—possibly similar to one you've discussed. Next write a rule that will help you remember how to figure out whether the verb should be singular or plural in sentences like the one you've composed.

Subject-Verb Agreement 2

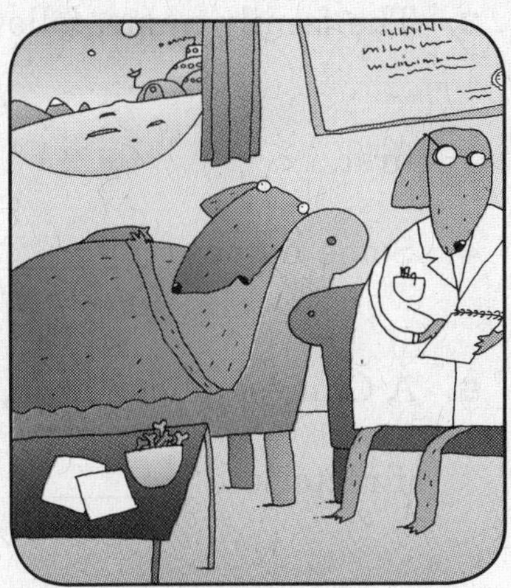

Figuring out whether a verb should be singular (to agree with a singular subject) or plural (to agree with a plural subject) can be tricky! Check out the examples and rules on pages 475, 508, and 509 in *Write Source* before completing the exercise below.

Examples

Subject Separated from the Verb:

I myself, not my friends, am responsible for the decisions I make.

(Make sure the subject and verb are in agreement.)

Subject Follows the Verb:

Piled on the table was a week's harvest of beans from Grandma's garden.

(Make sure the "true" subject and the verb agree.)

Indefinite Pronouns:

Everyone needs someone to talk to.

(The following indefinite pronouns require a singular verb: *each, either, neither, one, everyone, anyone, everybody, everything, someone, somebody, anybody, anything, nobody,* and *another*.)

Most of the ghost stories were scary, but none were truly frightening.

(The following indefinite pronouns can be either singular or plural: *all, any, most, none, some*. Check the noun the pronoun stands for to decide whether you need a singular or a plural verb.)

Write the correct form of the verb in each sentence below. The first sentence has been done for you.

1. Everyone in a traditional Chinese family *has* (*has, have*) three names, and each of those names is written using one character.

2. Each of the characters, which look like pictures, ____________ (*stands, stand*) for a particular part of the person's name.

3. The family name, followed by the person's given name, ___________ *(is, are)* written first.

4. Some names ___________ *(has, have)* a couple brush strokes, while others have many.

5. A Chinese phone book, quite different from English, Spanish, or German directories, ___________ *(lists, list)* names according to the number of brush strokes in the character representing the family name.

6. The names represented by the simplest characters with only a few brush strokes ___________ *(is, are)* listed near the beginning of the directory.

7. Anyone with a name requiring many brush strokes ___________ *(has, have)* to look for his or her listing near the end of the directory.

8. Everybody who wants to look up friends in the phone book ___________ *(has, have)* to remember more than 3,000 individual characters!

9. Perhaps anyone who grows up learning each word with a picture ___________ *(finds, find)* remembering Chinese characters as easy as remembering how a word sounds.

10. There ___________ *(is, are)* a number of other languages that use characters instead of letters, but Chinese is the most complex.

Next Step If you have problems remembering which indefinite pronouns are singular and which are plural, create a list for each type. Then use the first letters of the pronouns in each list to create an acronym to help you remember them as either singular or plural.

Subject-Verb Agreement 3

Subjects and verbs must agree in number in your sentences. A singular subject needs a singular verb. (The *book is* hidden.) Plural subjects require plural verbs. (The *books are* hidden.) It's also important to know which indefinite pronouns need a singular verb. Pronouns like *each, one,* and *everyone* require singular verbs. (See pages 475, 508, and 509 in *Write Source* for more information.)

Examples

Each of the boys hopes to find a fossil.

Either is capable of finding bones just like paleontologist Othniel Marsh.

Neither Jon nor Sherman expects to find a Brontosaurus bone.

In the following short paragraph, underline the subjects with a single line and their verbs with two lines. The first sentence has been done for you.

For a long time, no one realized that the Apatosaurus and the Brontosaurus were the same dinosaur. Different sets of dinosaur bones were found in different places in Wyoming and were thought to be from different dinosaurs. The first skeleton discovered had no skull. The American scientist Othniel Marsh named it Apatosaurus. Two years later, scientists found a more complete skeleton. Marsh named it Brontosaurus. Eventually, everyone realized that these two dinosaurs were the same. One of the names—Apatosaurus—has become formally accepted and is used by paleontologists. One of the names—Brontosaurus, the thunder lizard—seems to be more popular with the general public.

Subject-Verb Agreement 4

If the subject of a sentence is separated from its verb by other words or phrases, you may be tempted to make the verb agree with the closest noun—which is not necessarily the subject. One way to avoid this problem is to say the sentence aloud without the words that come between the subject and the verb. Try this technique on the examples below. (Also, see pages 508–509 and 728.1 in *Write Source* for more information.)

Examples

The raptors in the time of dinosaurs were fast and able hunters.

Fossil eggs found in the desert prove dinosaur mothers put their eggs in nests.

Read the sentences below. Then rewrite the sentences, separating the subject and the verb with a phrase. The first one has been done for you.

1. Raptors were hungry all the time.

   Raptors feeding on small animals were hungry all the time.

2. Dinosaurs lived millions of years ago.

3. Fossils tell us about dinosaurs.

4. Some dinosaurs were bigger than houses.

5. Tyrannosaurus Rex was the biggest meat eater.

Subject-Verb Agreement Review

Directions **In the following sentences, write the correct verb form in the blank and draw an arrow from the verb to its subject.**

1. The first people to use concrete for most of their public buildings ________ *(was, were)* the Romans.

2. Today, contractors ________ *(uses, use)* concrete for many purposes.

3. Sidewalks and streets in many cities ________ *(is, are)* concrete.

4. Most homeowners ___________ *(prefers, prefer)* durable concrete driveways.

5. A house builder using proper equipment ________ *(casts, cast)* concrete to look like brick.

6. Sometimes a contractor or a homeowner ________ *(adds, add)* color to the concrete.

7. With steel reinforcing rods, concrete buildings _______________ *(withstands, withstand)* the shock from an earthquake.

8. Under most houses with a basement _______ *(is, are)* a concrete floor.

9. Brick or wood, alternatives to concrete, ________ *(is, are)* usually more expensive.

10. Most of the airport runways in this country _______ *(is, are)* concrete.

11. In many towns in tornado alley, there ________ *(is, are)* concrete storm shelters.

12. The staff of the high school ___________ *(patrols, patrol)* five concrete playgrounds.

Sentence Problems Review 3

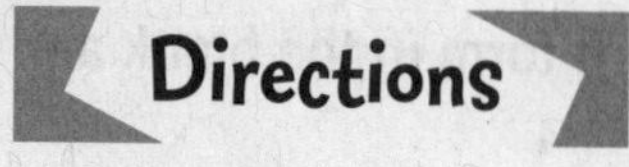

Read the paragraph below. It contains a number of words, phrases, and sentences that are unclear and could easily mislead the reader. Find one example of each type of error listed beneath the paragraph; write the number of the sentence in which you found each error on the blank provided. (See pages 503–510 in *Write Source* for help.) Then correct each error in the paragraph itself. (Rewrite the one sentence that needs major revising on the lines provided.)

(1) Learning to pilot a Superflooz VII Intergalactic Spacezipper at warp speed is really much easier than it sounds. **(2)** First, the pilot must strap into the control seat so he or she can't hardly move. **(3)** Then he must switch on the viewing screen. **(4)** This special screen nearly allows the pilot to see for 500 miles. **(5)** At this point, the pilot must switch on the Magno-Zip Atombooster. **(6)** This switch is located just above the pilot's head and looks sort of like a radish. **(7)** One of the switches are green and should not be touched at all, for it will activate the ship's destruct mechanism. **(8)** After warming up for three minutes, the pilot can throw the switch for the Magno-Zip Atombooster to the no-return position. **(9)** The pilot must remember not to overload their Magno-Zip Atombooster. **(10)** If the pilot follows one of these directions carefully, the trip should be a smooth one.

______ Double negative ______ Pronoun problem (agreement)

______ Misplaced modifier (one word) ______ Misplaced modifier (phrase)

______ Agreement of subject and verb

Revised Sentence: ____

____

Combining Sentences Using Key Words

Sometimes a single word can make a world of difference in a sentence. One added key word can provide just the extra touch needed to add impact to your sentence. If you have used two sentences to explain something, it's always a good idea to see if you can combine the two sentences by "borrowing" a key word from one and adding it to the other. Combining sentences by using key words can help you create more concise, mature sentences.

Examples

Combining with an Adjective:
John's brother nibbles "munchies" between meals. He is younger than John.
John's younger brother nibbles "munchies" between meals.

Combining with a Participle:
Ji's dog scares people. Ji's dog snarls.
Ji's snarling dog scares people.
(*Snarls* has been changed to its participle form.)

Combining with an Adverb:
I passed my English test. I passed it yesterday.
Yesterday, I passed my English test.

In each pair of sentences, underline the key word(s) in the second sentence and then move the form of that word (indicated in parentheses) to the first sentence.

1. Eligia did the exercises with ease. The exercises were difficult. *(adjective)*

   Eligia did the difficult exercises with ease.

2. I have to mow my overgrown lawn. I will mow the lawn later. *(adverb)*

   ____

3. The fans stormed onto the field. The fans screamed. *(participle)*

   ____

4. Juan wrote an essay on endangered species. It amazed everyone. *(participle)*

5. Jeison loves salsa. He loves it hot and spicy. *(adjective)*

6. The crowd loved the play. The crowd cheered. *(participle)*

7. I lost my wallet at the movies. I lost it last week. *(adverb)*

8. The sun made me squint. The sun was setting. *(participle)*

9. I changed the flat tire on the side of the road. I changed it quickly. *(adverb)*

10. Bill's basket saved the game for us. He made it at the last minute. *(compound adjective)*

Next Step Write five pairs of sentences suitable for key word combining. Exchange your sentences with a classmate. Each of you should combine the sentences you received.

Combining Sentences with a Series of Words or Phrases

Being able to combine shorter sentences into longer sentences is a very valuable writing skill to learn. Longer sentences can help you show relationships that are hard to express in shorter sentences. To effectively combine short sentences, you need to recognize what the shorter sentences have in common—what series of words, phrases, or ideas can be pulled together into one longer sentence. Study the examples below. (Also turn to pages 512 and 513 in *Write Source* for more examples.)

Examples

Shorter Sentences:
Aaron skies on snow.
He skies on water.
He skies on ice.

Combined Sentence Using a Series of Words:
Aaron skies on snow, water, and ice.

Shorter Sentences:
Aaron sprained his ankle.
He bruised his hip.
He wrenched his back.

Combined Sentence Using a Series of Phrases:
Aaron sprained his ankle, bruised his hip, and wrenched his back.

Combine the following sets of short sentences into longer ones using the method asked for in parentheses. The first one has been done for you.

1. John tore down the hill. He cut in front of Aaron. He caused him to fall. *(Use a series of phrases.)*

   John tore down the hill, cut in front of Aaron, and caused him to fall.

2. As Aaron tried to get out of John's way, he tumbled. Then he slid and spun. *(Use a series of words.)*

3. John was skiing too fast. He was moving carelessly from side to side. He was taking unnecessary chances. *(Use a series of phrases.)*

4. As John skied past Aaron, he whistled. He shouted and laughed. *(Use a series of words.)*

5. The ski patrol headed up the hill with their toboggan. They brought a back brace. They also brought an inflatable leg cast. *(Use a series of phrases.)*

6. Aaron now sits by himself. He watches hockey on television and dreams of getting back on the slopes. *(Use a series of phrases.)*

Next Step Write a paragraph describing an accident (or near accident) you have had. Then rewrite the paragraph to see how many sentences you can combine using a series of words or phrases as you did above. Compare your two paragraphs. Which one reads better?

Combining Sentences with Compound Subjects and Predicates

Sentences are not limited to having a single subject and predicate (or verb). A sentence can have two or more subjects called a **compound subject.** A sentence can also have a **compound predicate.** Some sentences may have both a compound subject and a compound predicate. Sometimes, instead of writing two short sentences, you may want to combine the subjects or predicates (or both) into a single sentence providing the same information. (See page 515 in *Write Source*.)

Note: Notice how using a compound predicate to combine the two sentences below eliminates repetition and lets you use one sentence instead of two.

Example

Shorter Sentences:
I got up at 6:00 in the morning.
I got dressed in my warmest clothes.

Combined Sentence Using a Compound Predicate:
I got up at 6:00 in the morning and dressed in my warmest clothes.

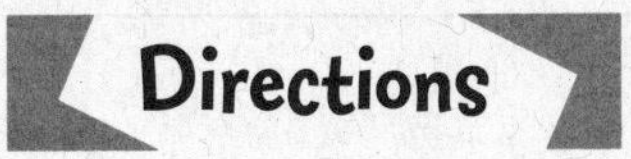

Combine each of the following pairs of sentences into a single sentence that uses compound subjects or predicates. See page 515 in *Write Source* for more information and additional examples. Some sentences may require both a compound subject and compound predicate. The first sentence has been done for you.

1. My dad was taking me ice fishing. My uncle was coming, too.
My dad and my uncle were taking me ice fishing.

2. My dad made me a huge pancake-and-sausage breakfast. He asked if I was full.

____

____

3. On the way to the lake, the two men told funny fishing stories. They poked fun at each other's fish tales.

4. I believed only about half the stories. I laughed at all of them anyway.

5. The heat in the car made me drowsy. The car's heat finally put me to sleep.

6. At the lake, the cold wind cut right through my warm clothes. It caused my teeth to start chattering.

7. My dad gathered kindling. My uncle helped and soon started a hot blazing fire.

8. I liked fishing that day. I enjoyed the warm fire even more.

Next Step Write a paragraph describing an experience you have had in nature. Then rewrite the paragraph, combining sentences using compound subjects and predicates. Compare your two paragraphs and discuss the results with a classmate. Do each of you see an improvement in your rewritten versions?

Kinds of Sentences

Sentences can be distinguished by their purpose. Some sentences ask questions (**interrogative**), some are statements (**declarative**), some give commands (**imperative**), and some are exclamations (**exclamatory**). As a writer, you choose the kind of sentence you want based on the message you want to give to the reader. (See page 518 in *Write Source* to examine the four kinds of sentences in more detail.)

Examples

Declarative Sentence:
Tornadoes are among the most destructive natural disasters.

Imperative Sentence:
Head for shelter immediately when a tornado warning is issued.

Interrogative Sentence:
Do you know where the safest place in your home is during a tornado?

Exclamatory Sentence:
The tornado caused millions of dollars of damage in just three minutes!

Directions

Label each of the following sentences as "declarative," "imperative," "interrogative," or "exclamatory." Then add the correct end punctuation. The first one has been done for you.

declarative **1.** Tornadoes occur most often in the Plains States during the spring and summer.

________ **2.** Tornado wind speeds can reach over 300 miles per hour

________ **3.** To protect yourself, learn all you can about tornadoes

________ **4.** The most violent tornadoes have more than one vortex or rotating center

________ **5.** Did you know that in Mississippi three 40-passenger buses were tossed over an eight-foot embankment during a tornado

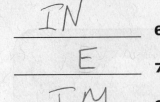

_______ **6.** Was anyone injured in the accident

_______ **7.** No, incredibly, no one was injured

_______ **8.** Stay away from windows and open spaces during a tornado

_______ **9.** Have you heard of "Tornado Alley"

_______ **10.** This is an area between Nebraska and central Texas where tornadoes are most likely to occur

_______ **11.** Most tornadoes happen during the month of May, but the most deadly ones occur in April

_______ **12.** If you find yourself in an open field during a tornado, find a low spot immediately

_______ **13.** A tornado can drive a piece of straw through a wooden post

_______ **14.** Tornadoes are most common in the United States, the former Soviet Union, and Australia

_______ **15.** If you are driving your car and the radio warns of a tornado in the area, what should you do

_______ **16.** Auntie Em, Auntie Em, it's a twister

Next Step Tornadoes, hurricanes, and earthquakes are frightening natural disasters. With a classmate, devise a safety plan for your home to deal with the natural disaster most likely to occur in your area of the country. Share that plan with your family. Be sure to check your writing for complete sentences.

Types of Sentences

Skilled writers vary the lengths of their sentences. Using too many short sentences makes writing choppy; however, using too many long sentences can make writing confusing. When you write, try to mix **simple, compound, complex,** and **compound-complex** sentences to achieve variety and clarity. (See pages 515–517 in *Write Source* for more on types of sentences.)

Examples

Simple Sentence:
Jack and Maria love in-line skating.

Compound Sentence:
They play on a roller-hockey team, and they enjoy the competition.

Complex Sentence:
Although they are amateurs now, Jack and Maria dream of being professional skaters someday.

Compound-Complex Sentence:
Because they are determined to fulfill their dream, Jack and Maria practice daily, and they read everything that they can find about skating.

Note: A compound-complex sentence contains two or more independent clauses and one or more dependent clauses.

Label the following sentences with "S" for simple, "C" for compound, "CX" for complex, and "CC" for compound-complex. The first sentence has been done for you.

S 1. Joseph Merlin, a Dutchman, invented roller skates in the eighteenth century.

_____ 2. After he studied the design of ice skates, Joseph fastened wooden spools in the place of the ice-skate blades.

SC 3. In 1763, metal wheels replaced the wooden spools, and in 1863, American inventor James Leonard Plimpton created rocking skates that allowed the skater to maneuver more easily.

C 4. Ball-bearing wheels were introduced late in the nineteenth century, and, as a result, roller-skating became even more popular.

S 5. Skateboards and in-line skates are modifications of roller skates.

CX 6. Skateboards are short, wide boards made of wood, plastic, or fiberglass.

C 7. In-line skates were first manufactured in the 1980s, and they have become very popular with people of all ages.

CX 8. Although roller-skating has not been accepted as an Olympic sport, athletes can compete in events like short-track speed skating with other roller skaters.

CC 9. Because Roller Derby was so popular in the 1950s, fans flocked to indoor rinks to watch, or they stayed home and watched on their televisions.

Next Step Find out more about Roller Derby, speed skating, or roller hockey by using the Internet or other sources. Write a paragraph about your findings and share your writing with a classmate. Ask your classmate to label the types of sentences you used in your paragraph.

Writing Complex Sentences 1

Sentence combining is one of the most valuable skills you can develop as a writer. With practice, you can combine short, choppy sentences into longer, smoother-reading sentences. One of the most efficient kinds of sentences to form when combining is the **complex sentence.** Complex sentences contain one independent clause and one or more dependent clauses. (See page 517 and 746.1 in *Write Source* for more information.)

Combine the following short sentences by adding the subordinating conjunction indicated in the parentheses. The first one has been done for you.

1. Visitors have been coming to Vancouver Island for years. Few know about the excellent surfing locations. *(although)*

Although visitors have been coming to Vancouver Island for years, few know about the excellent surfing locations.

2. The sun rose. Frank began to hike the trails. *(as soon as)*

The sun rose as soon as Frank began to hike th trails.

3. He planned to go hunting. He changed his plans so he could take his daughter skiing. *(although)*

Although he planned to go hunting, he changed his plans so he could take his daughter skiing.

4. People keep very busy and very fit on Vancouver Island. There are many outdoor activities. *(because)*

People keep very busy and very fit on Vancouver Island because there are many outdoor activities.

5. The hillsides are always green. It rains a lot on the coast. *(because)*

6. Residents of Vancouver Island are always prepared for rain or sunshine. The weather is unpredictable. *(because)*

7. Kayakers skim across the rivers. Skiers swish down the slopes. *(while)*

8. Vancouver Island is an excellent place to view killer whales. It is located on the Pacific coast. *(because)*

9. The tourists enjoyed a morning of whale watching. They visited the Parliament Building and had tea at the Empress Hotel. *(after)*

Next Step Write a paragraph about a place you would like to visit. Use short, simple sentences in your paragraph. Then exchange your paragraph with a classmate. Ask your classmate to revise your paragraph by combining the short sentences into complex sentences.

Writing Complex Sentences 2

Using adjective clauses to combine simple sentences will help you avoid unnecessary repetition in your writing. (Adjective clauses begin with words like *who, whose, which,* and *that.*) But be careful. Too many *who*'s or *which*'s will make your writing sound textbookish.

Who, whose, which, and **that** are called *relative pronouns.* See 706.3 in *Write Source* for a definition of relative pronouns and then write that definition below. (See page 517 and 746.1 for additional information.)

Definition: *A relative pronoun is both a . . .*

Example

Shorter Sentences:

The ancient oak was destroyed in the storm. It stood near the park entrance.

Combined Sentence Using an Adjective Clause:

The ancient oak that stood at the park entrance was destroyed in the storm.
("That stood at the park entrance" is an adjective clause that modifies "oak.")

Combine each pair of simple sentences into one complex sentence using "who," "which," or "that" as a connector.

1. The bearded wrestler gave his opponent a bear hug. The bearded wrestler was slick with sweat.

   The bearded wrestler, who was slick with sweat, gave his opponent a bear hug.

2. The night air revived him after his day in the fields. The air was cool and sweet smelling.

3. The construction workers were treated for heat exhaustion. They were building the new road through the park.

4. The sun is the center of our solar system. The sun is 93 million miles away.

5. The tracks led to the old miner's shack. The tracks were freshly made.

6. By the side of the road lay the ruined glider. It had been destined for Paris.

7. The agents escaped across the border. The agents set Mr. Goodwin free.

8. Rudy seldom goes to the weight room. He would rather jog than lift weights.

Next Step Many of the complex sentences you have made require commas. (The commas set off the adjective clause from the rest of the sentence.) Read about **restrictive** and **nonrestrictive clauses** on pages 584–585 in *Write Source* and check your sentences.

Writing Complex Sentences Review

Complex sentences are made up of an independent and a dependent clause. The independent clause in a complex sentence contains the most important idea in the sentence. The dependent clause contains a less important idea. The two clauses can be combined with a relative pronoun such as *who, whose, which,* or *that.* Clauses may also be combined with a subordinating conjunction such as *after, although, as, because, before, if, since, so, when, where, while, until, unless,* and so on.

Examples

Combining with a Relative Pronoun:
The writer is working on a new book. She has already published one book.
The writer, who has already published one book, is working on a new one.

Combining with a Subordinating Conjunction:
Carlos has started doing homework. He is getting better grades.
Since Carlos has started doing homework, he is getting better grades.

Note: When you are combining simple sentences into complex sentences, you may find it necessary to change an independent clause to a dependent clause. Examine the sentences carefully to see which clause is more important; then you'll know which clause (the less important one) can be subordinated.

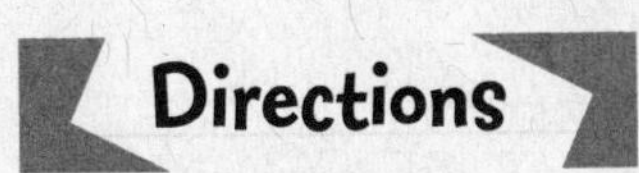

Combine each of the following pairs of sentences into one complex sentence. Refer to pages 517 and 746 in *Write Source*.

1. The writer's first book wasn't very popular. She was not discouraged.

   Although the writer's first book wasn't very popular, she was not discouraged.

2. Yi had faith in her ability. She started a new book immediately.

   ____

   ____

3. The publisher suggested that Yi write a book on her experiences in gymnastics. She had been a successful gymnast.

4. She thought the new book would be easy to write. It was on a topic familiar to her.

5. Yi felt comfortable writing about gymnastics. She had been a gymnast since age three.

6. Yi researched the topic. She discovered that gymnastics had changed considerably.

7. Yi has been working hard on her new book. She has not worried about her first book.

8. The publishers did not launch a nationwide promotional campaign immediately. They sensed outstanding sales potential.

Next Step Write a paragraph about an experience you had starting over after a first attempt failed. Then combine some of the sentences into complex sentences. Use a variety of dependent clauses. Make sure that the most important clause remains the independent clause.

Sentence Expanding

Successful writers have a knack for wording things the right way. They expand ideas with words and phrases that make their writing work. The smooth flow of their thoughts makes the actual words and sentences sound natural. (See pages 519–520 in *Write Source* for more examples.)

Details Added After the Basic Sentence:

He looks different, a little less like camp, a little more dressed up.

From *There's a Bat in Bunk Five* by Paula Danziger

Wil nodded to himself and slipped away, softly as a mouse, toward the back of the house where the tourists were never taken.

From "A Room Full of Leaves" by Joan Aiken

Details Added Before the Basic Sentence:

If his surroundings were gloomy and the company either boring to him or nonexistent, **he did not fidget.**

From "Total Stranger" by James Gould Cozzens

Details Added Before and After the Basic Sentence:

At the first sign of alarm, **he saw them clamber down the sapling and slip away** to the west beyond the gullberries.

From *The Yearling* by Marjorie Kinnan Rawlings

From then on, **it was like they were two dogs,** each waiting for the other one to make a move and start the fight.

From *Hoops* by Walter Dean Meyers

Study the sentences above. Read them out loud or have a partner read them to you. Listen carefully. Choose the two sentences you like best. On a separate piece of paper, write your own sentences, modeled after the professional writers' sentences. (To see how this is done, check out the example on pages 521–522 in *Write Source* under "Model Sentences.")

Directions **Expand the three basic sentences that follow by adding a variety of details that will result in more meaningful thoughts.**

1. Connie began to laugh.

2. Charles turned quickly.

3. Lakesha found the answer.

Next Step Refer to one of the short stories you've read in class, an article in your favorite magazine, or a section in one of your favorite books and copy down two expanded sentences that you really like. Underline the basic sentence and circle the words, phrases, and clauses that were used to expand it. Compare your findings with those of a classmate.

Expanding Sentences with Phrases

Experienced writers often combine short, simple sentences into longer, more meaningful ones by using a phrase in one of the sentences. The following types of phrases are often the key when it comes to sentence combining: **prepositional, participial, infinitive,** and **appositive phrases.** (See pages 512, 519, 520, and 730.3–730.4 in *Write Source* to read about these phrases as you work on the sentences that follow.)

Examples

Infinitive Phrase:
I watched to see it land.
("To see it land" is an infinitive phrase.)

Prepositional Phrase:
I watched from my bedroom window.
("From my bedroom window" is a prepositional phrase.)

Appositive Phrase:
I watched from my bedroom window, a great viewing place.
("A great viewing place" is an appositive phrase renaming "window.")

Participial Phrase:
Wondering about the bird, I watched from my bedroom window.
("Wondering about the bird" is a participial phrase describing "I.")

Combined Sentence:

Wondering about the bird, I watched from my bedroom window, a great viewing place, to see it land.

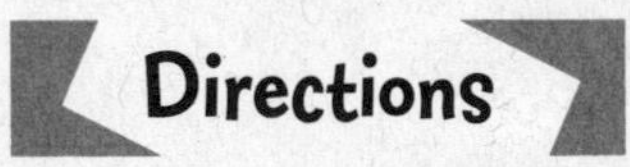

Combine each pair of simple sentences using the type of phrase indicated in the parentheses. The first sentence has been done for you.

1. The movie is scary. It is showing at the Hargrove Theater.
(participial phrase)

The movie showing at the Hargrove Theater is scary.

2. Frank and Phil waited for their pizza. They are the famous Fettucini brothers. *(appositive phrase)*

3. Glenna tore into a jelly-filled doughnut. It was from the "chewy and gooey" shelf in the bakery. *(prepositional phrase)*

4. Terrance studied each mountain bike. He wanted to determine which one would best meet his needs. *(infinitive phrase)*

5. Alex blew a hole in one of his basketball shoes. He was running down the court. *(participial phrase)*

6. Josie's hair can be uncontrollable. It is uncontrollable especially in wet weather. *("especially" + a prepositional phrase)*

7. The Girls Next Door played at the last school dance. They are music's answer to apple pie and sugar cookies. *(appositive phrase)*

Sentence Variety Review 1

Combining short, simple sentences into longer, more meaningful ones improves writing that otherwise sounds choppy. (See pages 511–522 in *Write Source* for more information.)

Combine the following set of four short sentences into longer, smoother-reading ones. Follow the sentence "frames" when they are provided for you.

Shorter Sentences:
Juan likes to race on his BMX bike.
Juan will be competing in races this summer.
He is hoping to win 30 races.
Then he can try to win the state title.

Frame 1: **Juan** ______________________________ bike,

therefore he ______________________________

and hoping ______________________________ ,

so that ______________________________ .

Frame 2: **Juan, who** ______________________________ ,

is hoping ______________________________

so that ______________________________ .

Frame 3: (Come up with your own version.)

____

____

____

____

____

Directions **Combine the following sets of simple sentences and then, on your own paper, finish the story. The first combined sentence has been done for you.**

1. Jerri thought tryouts were easier last year. She was in sixth grade then.

   Jerri thought tryouts were easier last year when she was in sixth grade.

2. She had thought for sure she had made the team. The coach had cut her.

3. She had wondered if Coach Anderson liked her. He sometimes yelled at her.

4. Jerri now thinks something different. Maybe the coach was trying to help her.

5. The practice lasted another 30 minutes. Coach Anderson stopped practice.

6. He told the players to take a shower. He told them to check the board on their way out. A list of players who made the second cut would be posted.

7. Jerri headed for the showers. She . . . (*Finish this story on your own paper.*)

Next Step Write a story about a situation that made you anxious. Exchange stories with a classmate. Check each other's work for choppiness. Correct or combine the sentences as necessary.

Sentence Variety Review 2

Use sentence-combining techniques to make each set of shorter sentences below into one longer sentence. Use the method indicated in parentheses at the end of each sentence to combine the sentences. Place your responses in the spaces provided. (For more information about sentence-combining techniques, see pages 511–514 in *Write Source*.)

1. Billy bowled three strikes. He bowled a split. *(Use a subordinating conjunction to make this a complex sentence.)*

   After Billy bowled three strikes, he bowled a split.

2. The match was long. The match was close. The match was exciting. *(Use a series of words.)*

3. Jess plays chess every day. Maria plays chess every day. *(Use a compound subject.)*

4. I went to bed early. I couldn't fall asleep. *(Use a compound sentence.)*

5. I always did my math homework. I still failed the exams. *(Use a compound verb.)*

6. The officer asked us to move along. The officer smiled. *(Use the participle "smiling.")*

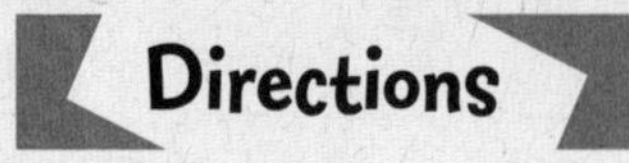

Combine each of the following sets of simple sentences into one complex sentence on the lines provided. The first sentence has been done for you.

1. Dan's right eye was twitching. He sat waiting for the test paper.

   Dan's right eye was twitching as he sat waiting for the test paper.

2. This was the last big English test of the term. Dan couldn't afford to fail it.

3. Dan had studied hard for the test. He still didn't feel confident.

4. Five minutes passed. Mr. Adams looked down Dan's row. He saw Dan just sitting there.

5. Dan couldn't write a single line. His mind was a complete blank.

6. Mr. Adams got up from his chair. He walked down the aisle toward Dan.

Next Step Complete the story on your own paper. Be ready to read aloud in class your startling conclusion to "The Testing of Dan."

Parts of Speech
Activities

Every activity includes a main practice section in which you learn about or review the different parts of speech. Most of the activities include helpful *Write Source* references. In addition, the **Next Step** activities give you follow-up practice with certain skills.

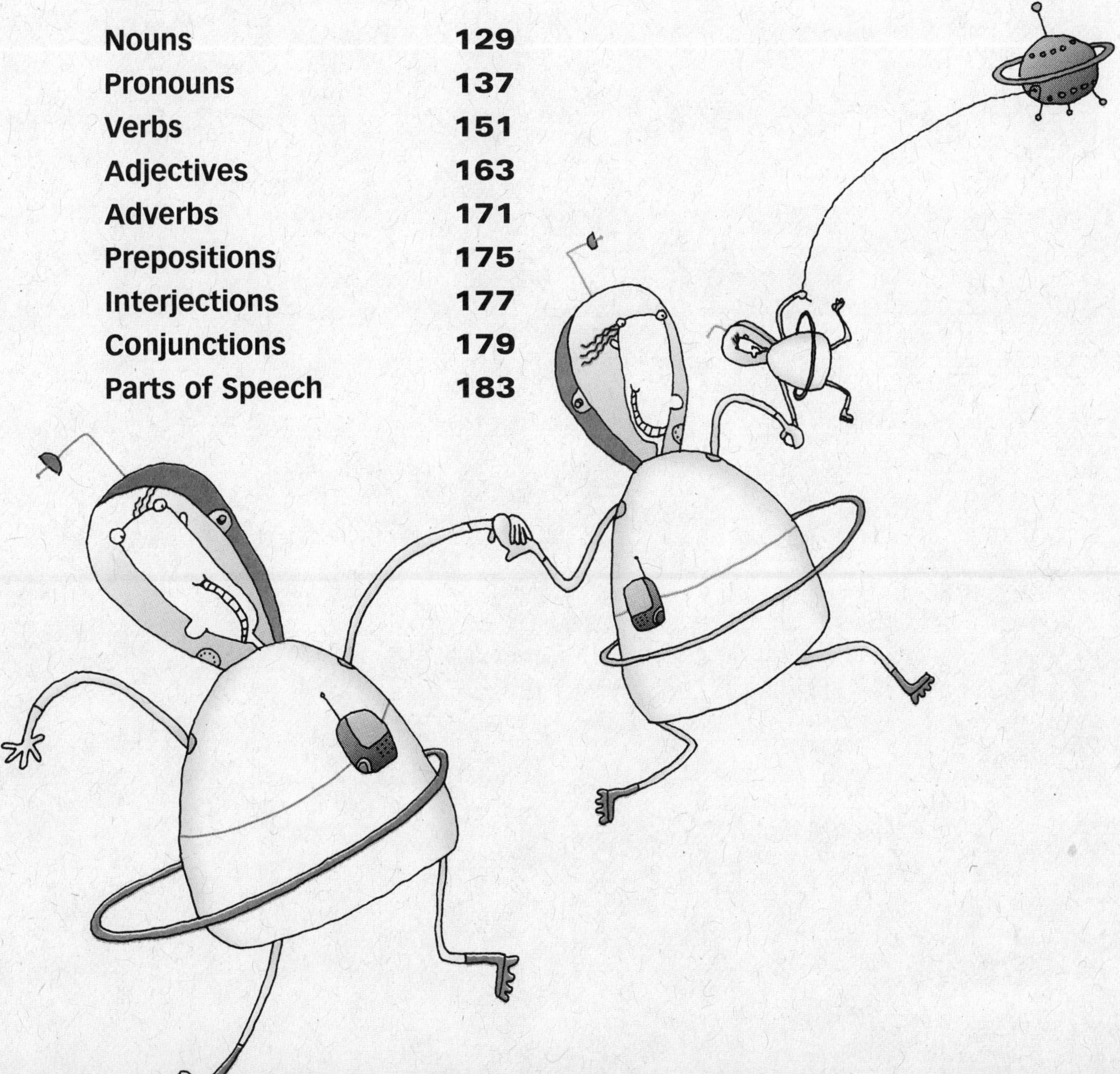

Common and Proper Nouns

A noun names a person, a place, a thing, or an idea. A **common noun** names any one of a group—not a specific person, place, thing, or idea. A common noun is *not* capitalized. A **proper noun** names a specific person, place, thing or idea. A proper noun is capitalized. (See 702.1 and 702.2 in *Write Source* for more information.)

Examples

Common Nouns	Proper Nouns
man	José
book	*American Heritage Dictionary*
city	Baltimore
team	Chicago Cubs

Underline the nouns in the sentences that follow. Write "C" above each common noun and "P" above each proper noun. The first sentence has been done for you.

1. The words [C] in our language [C] have been put into eight groups [C] called the parts [C] of speech [C].
2. A noun is the part of speech that names a person, a place, a thing, or an idea.
3. Common nouns name common things: roads, cars, teams, and so on.
4. Proper nouns are more specific: Avery Road, Ford, and New York Yankees.
5. Can you pick the proper nouns out of this list: Saturn, meteor, rainbow, *Apollo*, John Glenn, Labor Day?
6. Remember, common nouns name common things and are not capitalized; proper nouns name specific things and are capitalized.

Directions Study the two lists of nouns that follow. Then add three nouns to each list. Make sure your nouns fit with the rest of the words in each list.

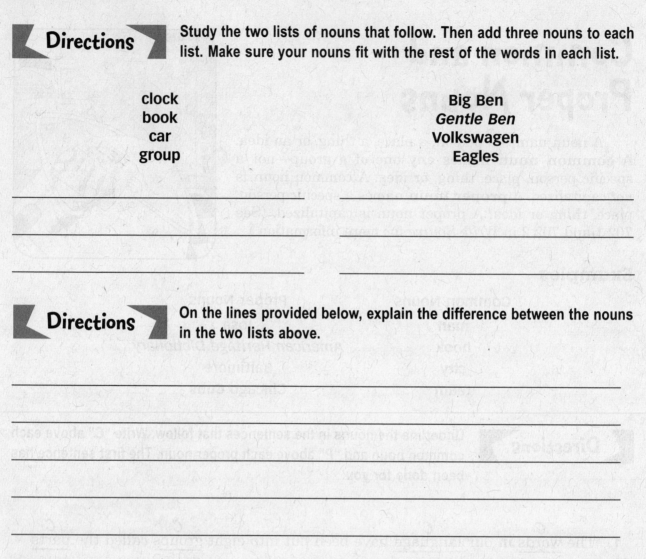

clock	Big Ben
book	*Gentle Ben*
car	Volkswagen
group	Eagles
______________	______________
______________	______________
______________	______________

Directions On the lines provided below, explain the difference between the nouns in the two lists above.

____

____

____

____

____

Note: Share your explanation with one of your classmates. Then compare it with the explanations in *Write Source* at 702.1 and 702.2. How close does your explanation match the ones in the book?

Next Step Select one noun from the first list at the top of this page (*clock* through *group*) as the beginning of a concrete poem or an acrostic poem. (See page 359 in *Write Source* for help with your poem.)

Concrete and Abstract Nouns

Ask my brother to wash dishes, and he'll answer, "Get real!" Actually, dirty dishes are "real" enough. You can see them, feel them—maybe even smell them! **Concrete nouns** name physical things like those dishes. But what if you can't see or touch something? Is love "real"? Of course it is. **Abstract nouns,** such as "love" and "poverty," name things that you can think about but can't see or touch. (See 702.3 and 702.4 in *Write Source* for more information.)

Underline all the words used as nouns in the sentences that follow. Then put a "C" above each concrete noun and an "A" above each abstract noun. Some words are tricky! They may name either a concrete or an abstract concept. The first sentence has been done for you.

1. When we gaze at stars (C), we are looking into the distant past (A), because the light (C) from stars (C) takes many years (A) to travel to Earth (C).
2. Some dinosaurs half-buried their eggs in mud, then covered the tops with rotting vegetation to warm them.
3. It is an amazing fact that giant redwoods transport water tremendous distances from their roots to their leaves without a pump.
4. By performing a dance, a honeybee can tell other workers in the hive where flowers filled with nectar can be found.
5. Hummingbirds are not shy; if you wear red clothes, they will fly close enough to get a careful look at you.
6. The Constitution guarantees all Americans basic freedoms.
7. It was not easy for the original 13 colonies to win those freedoms.
8. In fact, many colonists did not like the idea of a rebellion against England.

9. Some continued to declare their loyalty to King George.

10. The Eiffel Tower reminds me of drawings in my geometry book.

11. At the basketball game, one of the players had to leave the game because of an injury.

12. He sprained his ankle when he stepped on someone else's foot.

13. The teams showed good sportsmanship even when the spectators were a little rude.

14. Emilio went through a growth spurt last year.

15. Now his dream is to play football in high school.

Next Step Share the results of your work with a classmate. Discuss any differences you may find. Talk about ways you can distinguish between abstract and concrete nouns, and write your guidelines in the space below.

Subject and Object Nouns

Every word in a sentence has a job to do. Nouns do more than just *name* a person, a place, a thing, or an idea. The specific job a noun does in a sentence depends on where it is used and how it is related to the other words. (See 704.4–704.7 in *Write Source*.)

Examples

Subject Noun:

Our family loved spending afternoons in the park.

(A *subject noun* names the person, place, thing, or idea that is doing the action or is being talked about: "family" is a subject noun.)

Predicate Noun:

Our favorite game was football.

(A *predicate noun* follows a linking verb or a form of the *be* verb—*is, are, was, were*—and repeats or renames the subject: "football" renames *game.)*

Possessive Noun:

My family's favorite lunch was pizza.

(A *possessive noun* is a noun that shows ownership: "family's" is a possessive noun.)

Object Noun:

We would often eat our lunch there.

(A noun becomes an *object noun* when it is used as the direct object, indirect object, or object of the preposition: "lunch" is a direct object.)

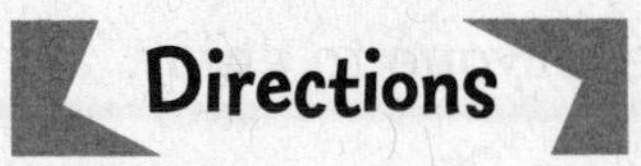

Label each underlined noun in the following sentences. Use "SN" for subject noun, "PN" for predicate noun, "POS" for possessive noun, "ON" for object noun. The first two sentences have been done for you.

SN **1.** The small park in my neighborhood used to be my favorite place.

ON **2.** My mother took me to the park almost every day.

_____ **3.** I chased squirrels and pigeons around the huge trees.

_____ **4.** My mother gave me ice cream and other treats.

_____ **5.** Kids from all over the city's south side gathered in the park.

_______ **6.** Parents sat and talked on benches while the kids played on the equipment.

_______ **7.** Old people came and played chess and checkers on stone tables in the sun.

_______ **8.** City police officers patrolled the park on their bicycles.

_______ **9.** The police officers were part of the fun.

_______ **10.** One police officer even gave me an ice-cream cone.

_______ **11.** Last summer many city workers went on strike.

_______ **12.** In just a few days, the park was a total disaster.

_______ **13.** People discarded paper and litter on the grass and playground.

_______ **14.** Parents didn't want their kids playing in a bunch of garbage.

_______ **15.** The park had been a green oasis in the city's concrete desert.

_______ **16.** Neighborhood residents organized a clean-up-the-park campaign.

_______ **17.** On the designated day, practically the whole neighborhood showed up for work.

_______ **18.** People swept, raked, and picked up all the garbage in the park.

_______ **19.** Four ladies from our building planted flowers along the park's walkway.

_______ **20.** The park was once again a wonderful place for everyone to enjoy.

Next Step Write a paragraph describing a time when people joined together to accomplish something. It might be a neighborhood project or something done in school. Where the activity took place doesn't really matter. What matters is that you describe something that people thought needed to be done and got together to do. You might even want to write about something that you did with members of your own family.

Specific Nouns

Specific nouns are especially helpful when you are trying to create a clear image or word picture for a reader. Notice the difference between the two example sentences below. The first sentence contains general nouns, and it doesn't express a very clear idea. The second sentence, which includes more specific nouns, does express a clear idea. (See page 471 in *Write Source* for more information.)

The scientist wanted to study animals in another country. (general nouns)

Jane Goodall wanted to study chimpanzees in Tanzania. (specific nouns)

Look at the examples below. Notice that the nouns move from very general at the top to very specific at the bottom. By using a good number of specific nouns in your writing, you will make it easier for the reader to understand exactly what you are saying.

Examples

person	place	thing	idea
man	building	book	pain
artist	arena	reference book	headache
Vincent van Gogh	Madison Square Garden	Farmers' Almanac	migraine

Now think of three nouns for each of the categories below. Each noun you add must be more specific than the one before it, as in the examples above.

person	place	thing	idea

Example

The <u>car</u> drove past the <u>building</u>.

a. *The foreign car drove past the government building.*

b. *The Toyota convertible drove past the White House.*

Directions **Revise each of the following sentences twice. Make sentence B even more specific than sentence A. (Add or change other words as necessary to create a better sentence.)**

1. The **animal** is in the **building.**

a. ______

b. ______

2. The **doctor** performed the **operation.**

a. ______

b. ______

3. The **singer** was given an **award.**

a. ______

b. ______

4. A **relative** came down with an **illness.**

a. ______

b. ______

5. The **dog** ran around the **tree.**

a. ______

b. ______

Pronouns and Antecedents

You always want to write so your readers clearly understand what it is you're trying to say. You also must make sure that the antecedent of a pronoun (the word the pronoun refers to) is clear in your writing. (For more information, see 706.1 in *Write Source.*)

Example

Unclear Pronoun Use:

I took my car to the corner gas station because it was nearly empty.
(This sentence does not clearly state *what* was nearly empty—the car or the gas station—because the antecedent of the pronoun "it" is unclear.)

Clear Pronoun and Antecedent:

Because my car was nearly empty, I took it to the corner gas station.
("Car" is definitely the antecedent of the pronoun "it" in this sentence.)

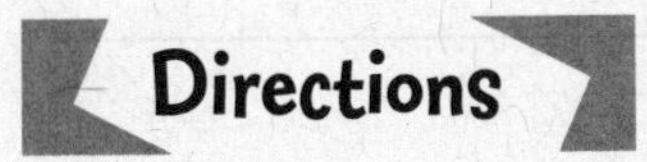

Rewrite each of the following sentences so that the pronoun has a clearly stated antecedent. Be sure to use the boldfaced pronoun in your new sentence. The first sentence has been done for you.

1. Reggie sat in the first row of the theater since **it** was empty.

   Since the first row of the theater was empty, Reggie sat in it.

2. When I put my foot into the shoe, **it** was wet.

3. When the ice floe reached the old dam, **it** broke.

4. After he'd left the present on the doorstep, Gerard realized **it** was the wrong one.

5. Though the chauffeur drove the limousine into the fence, **it** wasn't damaged.

6. I can't give the bone to my dog because **it** is too sharp.

7. I don't go to movies with my young cousins because **they** are too violent. (*they* becomes *them*)

8. Traffic, on the way to my aunt's dinner, **which** was terrible, made us late.

Next Step Turn to page 714 in *Write Source* to find a chart of singular and plural personal pronouns. Write at least three sentences that use a pronoun with its antecedent. Draw an arrow from the pronoun to its antecedent.

Types of Pronouns 1

Pronouns do a great job of standing in for nouns. But some pronouns do more: *Reflexive* and *intensive* pronouns, for example, give their antecedents extra emphasis.

Another group of pronouns—*indefinite pronouns*—also stand in for nouns, but they don't refer to a definite person or thing. Indefinite pronouns are often used without antecedents. Indefinite pronouns keep the subject vague—which might be a relief to the person who is the subject: *Somebody* spilled the cereal. *Nobody* cleaned it up. *Somebody* left the bike in the driveway. (See 708.2, 708.3, and 710.1 in *Write Source* for more information.)

Examples

Reflexive Pronoun:

Little Jeff has finally learned how to dress himself.

(The reflexive pronoun "himself" throws the action back on the subject of the sentence. The sentence would not be complete without it.)

Intensive Pronoun:

Little Jeff himself put on his pants.

(The intensive pronoun "himself" intensifies or emphasizes its antecedent. However, it's not necessary; the sentence is complete without it.)

Indefinite Pronoun:

Somebody left these pants on the floor.

(The indefinite pronoun "somebody" doesn't stand in for a particular person. The person is indefinite or unknown.)

Write a reflexive, intensive, or indefinite pronoun in the blanks in the sentences below. Write "Ref" above each reflexive pronoun, "Int" above each intensive pronoun, and "Ind" above each indefinite pronoun. The first sentence has been done for you.

1. ___Ind Something___ warned me not to make a sound as I tiptoed up the dark staircase.

2. Instead, I ended up making loud creaking sounds as if King Kong __________ were stomping up to the second story.

3. I could not stop ______________ from trembling like a leaf.

4. As I reached the top of the stairs, I felt ______________ brush my leg, and then I heard it throw ______________ down the stairs.

5. I stood as if frozen to the landing, desperately telling ______________ to calm down.

6. As my eyes adjusted to the darkness, I looked around for ______________ to hide behind.

7. Just then, I saw ______________ with many shining eyes watching me from under the bed.

8. I threw ______________ in the direction of the light switch.

9. I flipped the switch and found ______________ face-to-face with a possum and her brood.

10. ______________ could have prepared me for what I saw next: the possum family suddenly appeared to be dead.

11. Thinking of ______________ as a murderer, I carried the throw rug full of "dead" possums out to the garden.

12. Later, when I took Mom out to the garden, ______________—not one possum—was there.

13. Much later I realized that ______________ had ever told me what "playing possum" really meant.

Next Step Write a short story about a scary experience you actually had or about a scary experience someone told you about. Try to use at least one reflexive pronoun, one intensive pronoun, and one indefinite pronoun in your story. Exchange papers with a friend. Enjoy the story and then check to see if the pronouns have been used correctly.

Types of Pronouns 2

Review the special types of pronouns listed below. Notice how each type functions. It might be to ask a question, to point out something, or to relate a subordinate clause to a main clause. (See pages 706.3, 706.4, and 708.1 in *Write Source* for more information.)

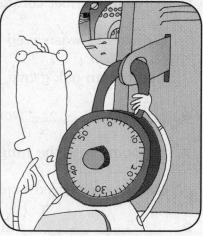

Examples

Relative Pronouns:

Wolves are not just wild dogs that can be tamed.
("That" refers back to "dogs" and links the underlined subordinate clause to the main clause of the sentence.)

Interrogative Pronouns:

To whom did you give your locker combination?
(An interrogative pronoun asks a question. Use "who," "whose," or "whom" when asking questions about people. Use "which" and "what" when asking about things or ideas.)

Demonstrative Pronouns:

These seeds will sprout, but those are old and rotten.
(A demonstrative pronoun points out a thing or an idea without naming it.)
Note: It is incorrect to pair demonstrative pronouns with "here" or "there," such as "This here book . . . ".

Write a pronoun in the blank in each sentence below. Write "I" above interrogative pronouns, "D" above demonstrative pronouns, and "R" above relative pronouns. The first sentence has been done for you.

1. The sky filled with an eery glow, ___R which___ we suddenly realized was fire!

2. The mall parking lot was full of snowy mounds, ________________ only an hour before had been cars of many shapes and colors.

3. The contractor knows how to select paint ________________ will be durable under wet or moist conditions.

4. ________________ is a mountain pass that an experienced climber could make, but ________________ is a deadly crevasse no one could get through.

5. After its 40-foot columns rotted, a 200-year-old building at Oxford University was saved because its original builder, planning ahead, had planted an oak grove ________ provided the replacement columns.

6. ________ word game would you like to play?

7. Stepping into the jungle ________ grew in a thick, thorny tangle, the inexperienced explorer was instantly lost.

8. ________ animal is a crocodile, and ________ is an alligator.

9. If you had to list the 10 most important inventions of the twentieth century, ________ would they be?

10. The field, ________ was still wet from yesterday's rain, turned into a muddy mess by halftime.

11. Mr. Lawrence, ________ the students secretly nicknamed Lumpy, was known for his huge midafternoon snacks.

12. ________ cotton jerseys are comfortable, but ________ wool ones are scratchy.

13. The coach, ________ job hinged on winning the last two games of the season, looked very nervous.

14. ________ country produces more oil, Mexico or Venezuela?

Next Step Find an interesting story in a newspaper. Circle the relative pronouns, underline the demonstrative pronouns, and put brackets around the interrogative pronouns. Before you start, guess which type of pronouns will be used most. Count the circles, underlines, and brackets when you are finished. Was your guess correct?

Uses of Pronouns

Just like the nouns they replace, pronouns can be subjects or objects in a sentence. Possessive pronouns can also stand in for possessive nouns. Most of the time, using the correct form of the pronoun isn't a problem. But sometimes, substituting a pronoun for a noun can result in confusion.

As you review the examples below, you'll notice that many problems with pronouns happen because people write the way they talk. (See 710.1 and 714.2 in *Write Source* for more information.)

Examples

Incorrect:

Everyone has their own ticket.

("Their" is plural and does not match its singular antecedent, "everyone.")

Correct:

Everyone has his or her own ticket.

("His or her" is singular. It now matches its singular antecedent, "everyone.")

Note: When it's not clear if the pronoun should be male or female, use the phrase "his or her."

Incorrect:

When Joan and Sharone were neighbors, she souped up her BMX bike.

Correct:

When Joan was Sharone's neighbor, she souped up Sharone's BMX bike.

Incorrect:

If someone sprains a knee, you will need physical therapy.

("Someone" is a third-person subject. "You" is a second-person subject. The pronouns need to be in the same person or else it is not clear whose knee is sprained.)

Correct:

If someone sprains a knee, he or she will need physical therapy.

Incorrect:

John he makes great chili.

(Avoid using a pronoun immediately following a noun.)

Correct:

John makes great chili.

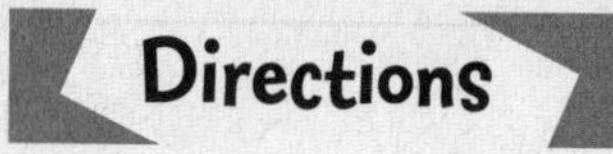

Correct the common pronoun errors in the sentences below by rewriting the sentences in the spaces provided. Be prepared to discuss why you made the corrections. The first sentence has been done for you.

1. Sue's dog, Voltaire, he likes to play soccer, but they often play too rough.

   Sue's dog, Voltaire, likes to play soccer, but he often plays too rough.

2. I don't suppose you thought about a person's feelings when you took my sweater and stretched it out, and then gave it back to that person without having it cleaned.

3. Soon, if an athlete injures their knee, doctors will be able to repair the sinews with a synthetic material that is twice as strong as their original muscle.

4. If a student wants to participate in extracurricular sports, you have to maintain a passing grade point average.

Next Step In one of the books you are reading, find a paragraph that uses a number of pronouns. Then list the pronouns on a sheet of paper and identify each one as either (1) a subject pronoun, (2) an object pronoun, or (3) a possessive pronoun. If you find an odd use that doesn't seem to fit the basic rules, ask your teacher for help.

Pronoun-Antecedent Agreement 1

One of the most important rules of writing is this one: *A pronoun must agree with its antecedent.*

Here's what the rule means: Every time you use a pronoun in place of a noun, you must be sure that the pronoun is the same number (singular or plural) and the same person (first, second, third) as the original noun. (For more information, see 706.1 in *Write Source.*)

Example

The four deer scattered as the skunk approached them.
(A pronoun must agree in number with its antecedent. Because the noun "deer" is plural, the pronoun "them" must also be plural.)

Cross out the incorrect pronouns in the following sentences. Write corrections above them. The first one has been done for you.

1. My grandma rolled her eyes when she heard ~~they~~ *she* can buy eggs laid by vegetarian chickens that don't eat bugs or meat by-products.
2. Grandma always thought having chickens eat bugs was good for it.
3. Grandma says that when she was growing up, kids were expected to eat whatever was put in front of you, and so were chickens.
4. "Things change," I said. "When IBM started in the '50s, he thought five computers throughout the world would be enough to do the job."
5. My grandma said her doesn't see what computers have to do with chickens.
6. I pointed out that computers are used to coordinate the shipping of fruits and vegetables, making it available throughout the world any time of the year.
7. Grandma said we should ask a chicken if they like fruits and vegetables before we make them eat this food.

8. "Not chickens, Grandma—people demand special eggs, because he's gotten used to foods from all over the world," I explained.

9. My grandma says they know what they would do if somebody started demanding special eggs at their house.

10. Grandma would plunk that peanut butter jar down on the table and invite her guest to make themself a sandwich.

11. "What if a person eats a special diet for their health?" I asked.

12. As long as she doesn't have to cook it, Grandma supposes a person can eat whatever he or she wants.

13. A person should mind their manners, Grandma says.

14. A guest should eat what they're served.

15. People shouldn't make unreasonable demands on the hostess even if it's important to stay on her diets.

16. People should thank the cook, Grandma says, even if him meal is terrible!

Next Step Write a story about something your grandmother or grandfather says (or base your story on a fictional grandmother or grandfather). Try to use a few pronouns in your story. Underline your pronouns and circle their antecedents. Check that the pronouns agree in number and in person with their antecedents.

Pronoun-Antecedent Agreement 2

Do you sometimes need an "antecedent detector"? You will need to develop your own sense of what makes pronouns and their antecedents clear and easy to read. Rewriting poorly written sentences—like the ones below—will help you develop this sense and, in turn, help you become a better writer. (For more information, see 706.1 and 706.3 in *Write Source*.)

Example

Confusing Pronoun Reference:

As I dug into my meal, Karen stuck her gum on my plate, which tasted as good at it looked.

Corrected Sentence:

As Karen stuck her gum on my plate, I dug into my meal, which tasted as good as it looked.

Directions **Find the confusing pronoun references in the sentences below. Then, rewrite each sentence on the lines below it. The first sentence has been done for you.**

1. Most kids appreciate a practical joke, especially if they are a little bit crazy.

   Most kids appreciate a practical joke, especially if it is a little bit crazy.

2. Jack's dad took us for ice cream after the game, while he was bragging about how he made the three-point shot that won the game.

3. As I looked out the bedroom window, a doe ran behind our truck, but it moved before I could grab my camera.

4. At sunrise in the mountains, the campers were able to ignore their aching muscles and sore feet because they were so beautiful.

5. The Scouts had been hiking so long in the mountains that they were worn down.

6. Lots of buses stop in front of the school to pick up students, all of them smelling like diesel fuel.

7. I picked up some pretzels when I went for a walk with my dogs, and I ate them.

8. I helped dry towels with my sisters, by hanging them on the clothesline.

Next Step Write down a verse from a song—a traditional song or a song you've heard on the radio. Circle the pronouns. Draw a line from each pronoun to its antecedent. Are all the antecedents clear?

Action, Linking, and Helping Verbs

I'd saved up for months for my trip to the Super Bowl. The game electrified the crowd. My favorite team won in overtime. But when a reporter asked me what I thought of the game, I could think of only one word: "Awesome!" A few vivid action verbs that afternoon would have saved my big TV moment. Action verbs can also save your writing, turning it from dull to exciting. (See page 718 in *Write Source* for more information.)

Examples

Linking Verbs:
You could be a radio programmer and broadcaster.

Action Verbs:
You could create and broadcast your own radio program.
(In this sentence, "could" is a helping verb.)

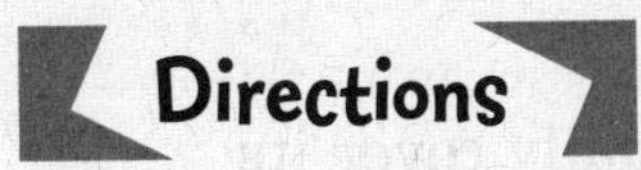

Underline the verbs twice in each of the following sentences. (Don't forget to underline helping verbs as well.) Label each action verb with an "A" and each linking verb with an "L." The first sentence has been done for you.

1. Some recent movies and television shows dramatize (A) the danger of asteroids to life on Earth.

2. Some scientists feel that at least one huge asteroid smashed into Earth during the time that dinosaurs roamed the planet.

3. Under the ocean near Mexico's Yucatan Peninsula lies an impact crater nearly 180 kilometers wide.

4. Scientists believe an asteroid crashed there 65 million years ago and raised a cloud of dust and ash that cooled Earth and killed the dinosaurs.

5. While another asteroid strike like that might not destroy the human race, it could wreck our civilization.

6. Asteroids orbit the sun in a "belt" between Mars and Jupiter.

7. Sometimes the gravity of those planets nudges an asteroid out of the belt, and it crosses Earth's orbit.

8. Normally Earth's gravity then swings the asteroid farther toward the sun, where it disintegrates.

9. Earth has several large craters, however, where asteroids have struck in the past.

10. Because the moon has no atmosphere, impact craters actually cover its surface.

11. Most asteroid strikes happened long, long ago, during the fury of the solar system's formation.

12. In fact, the chance that a major asteroid will strike Earth is very, very small.

13. Still, a number of government agencies watch the skies for "killer" asteroids.

14. Even though the chance of a deadly strike is slim, "Better safe than sorry."

Next Step Write a paragraph describing an event you witnessed: a concert, a parade, a game. Use action verbs to make your paragraphs come to life for the reader.

Simple Verb Tenses

A verb does more than express an action or link the subject to another word in a sentence. A verb also expresses tense, or time. A good place to begin a study of verb tenses is with the three simple tenses: **present, past,** and **future.** (See page 720 in *Write Source* for more information.)

Examples

Present Tense:
John walks up to me, his backpack dragging on the ground.

Past Tense:
John walked up to me, his backpack dragging on the ground.

Future Tense:
John will walk up to me, his backpack dragging on the ground.

Underline the verb twice in each of the following sentences. Then put each sentence in a different "time zone." That is, rewrite each sentence twice, using the verb in all three simple tenses. (Also, underline the verbs with two lines in your new sentences.) The first one has been done for you.

1. **Present:** *My battery-driven car bumps into the furniture.*

   Past: *My battery-driven car bumped into the furniture.*

   Future: *My battery-driven car will bump into the furniture.*

   ____

2. **Present:** ______________________________

   ____

   Past: *I called the folks at the AAA auto club to help me.*

   Future: ______________________________

   ____

3. **Present:** ______

Past: ______

Future: *In two minutes flat, the person from AAA will start my car.*

4. **Present:** *Mikey balances two dozen paperbacks on his head at once.*

Past: ______

Future: ______

5. **Present:** ______

Past: *The books slid off in all directions.*

Future: ______

6. **Present:** ______

Past: ______

Future: *The class will laugh uproariously.*

Next Step Write one sentence about your last summer. Now put it in present and future tenses. Write one sentence about your next summer. Then rewrite it in past and present tenses.

Irregular Verbs

The principal parts of a verb are the **present tense,** the **past tense,** and the **past participle.** While the past principal parts of most verbs are created simply by adding "ed" to the main verb (*like, liked, liked*), the different parts of irregular verbs follow no set pattern (*run, ran, run; bite, bit, bitten*). This makes it more challenging to use the principal parts correctly in your writing. The following activity—and *Write Source*—can help. (See page 722 in *Write Source* for a chart of irregular verbs.)

Directions A good way to learn these irregular verbs is simply to say them over to yourself several times. They have a certain rhythm that helps to make them stick in your mind. Try these easier ones first. Look at them and say them to yourself several times.

Present Tense	Past Tense	Past Participle
begin	began	begun
bite	bit	bitten
drink	drank	drunk
see	saw	seen
write	wrote	written

Of course, there are many more troublesome verbs, including the following:

bring	brought	brought
burst	burst	burst
drown	drowned	drowned
swing	swung	swung
wake	woke	woken

Directions Now try to fill in the blanks below with the principal parts of the verbs you just studied. Try to do it without looking!

begin		
drink		
write		
swing		
drown		

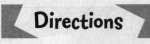

Now turn to the chart of irregular verbs on page 722 in *Write Source*. Read it slowly to yourself. Listen as a classmate reads it to you. Make note of the verbs that cause you trouble. Study those. Then close your book and fill in the chart that follows. (Check your work when you finish.)

Present Tense	Past Tense	Past Participle
am, be		
	bit	
	brought	
catch	caught	
come	came	
	did	
draw		
eat	ate	
fall		
fight		
fly		
		known
lie (recline)		
set		
		shaken
	swam	

Next Step Use the most troublesome verbs (from the list above) in a paragraph. Here's a possible starting point:

I brought a water balloon to the picnic, and it . . .

Perfect Tenses

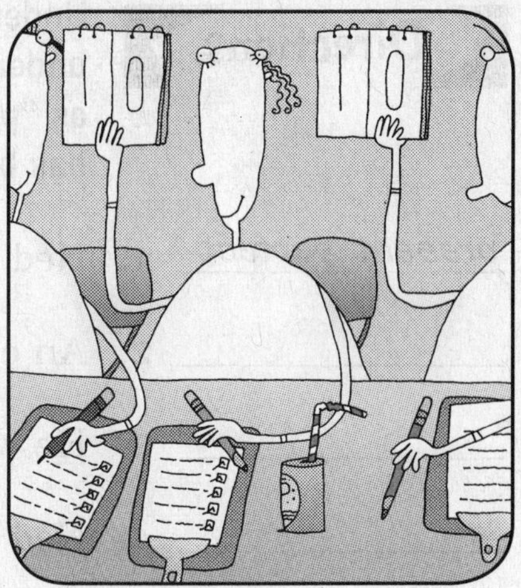

At times, the action you want to express isn't clearly a present, past, or future action. For example, let's say that you began cleaning your messy locker five days ago and you are still cleaning it. Your cleaning is neither a past action nor a present action. Instead, it is an ongoing action. In this type of situation, you need to use one of the three perfect tenses to state the action. Note the use of the perfect tenses in the following sentences. The verb in each sentence is in color. (See 724.1–724.3 in *Write Source* for more examples.)

Examples

Present Perfect Tense:
The amusement park has remained my favorite place to spend a summer day.

Past Perfect Tense:
Before this year, the Monster ride had frightened me.

Future Perfect Tense:
After this summer, I will have visited the park for six straight years.

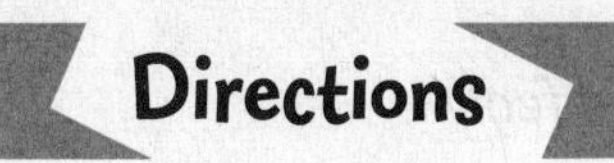

Directions **Using *Write Source*, answer the following questions about the perfect tenses.**

1. A verb in the *present perfect tense* expresses action that ____________________
____
____

2. A verb in the *past perfect tense* expresses action that ____________________
____
____

3. A verb in the *future perfect tense* expresses action that ____________________
____

Directions **Underline the verb twice in each of these sentences. Don't forget to underline helping verbs as well. In the space provided, label each verb as "present perfect," "past perfect," or "future perfect." The first one has been done for you.**

present perfect **1.** Ned Frap, the ruler of the planet, has escaped in a spacepod.

__________ **2.** An earthquake had leveled his plastic dome.

__________ **3.** He will have used all his energy pellets before nightfall.

__________ **4.** Ned had lived in his dome for six years.

__________ **5.** In those six years, he had never gone outside.

Directions **Underline the verb twice in each of the following sentences. Then rewrite each sentence by changing the verb to the tense indicated in parentheses. Remember that all perfect tenses are composed of a form of *have* plus the past participle of the main verb. The first one has been done for you.**

1. The Phantom Blur prepares very carefully for the mission. *(present perfect)*

The Phantom Blur has prepared very carefully for the mission.

2. He sneaks into embassies, castles, and prisons. *(present perfect)*

____

3. Tomorrow, the Phantom Blur will attempt a new mission. *(future perfect)*

____

4. At first, he considered the mission a pushover. *(past perfect)*

____

5. Perhaps by tomorrow night he will change his mind. *(future perfect)*

____

Transitive and Intransitive Verbs

There are two types of action verbs—transitive and intransitive. **Transitive** verbs "transfer" their action to a direct object (and sometimes to an indirect object). The direct object completes the meaning of the sentence, as in the examples that follow. An **intransitive** verb completes its meaning without an object. (See 728.2, 728.3, and 730.1 in *Write Source* for more information.)

Examples

Transitive Verb:

The teacher handed me the extinguisher.

A **direct object** receives the direct action of the verb. It answers the question *who* or *what* after the verb. The teacher handed me what? ("extinguisher"—direct object)

An **indirect object** is indirectly affected by the verb. It tells *to whom* or *for whom* something is done. The teacher handed the extinguisher to whom? ("me"—indirect object)

Intransitive Verb:

Everyone in our class walked quietly down the hall.

An intransitive verb does not need to transfer its action to a direct object to complete the thought. In this sentence, the verb "walked" is intransitive and does not have a direct object.

Write "T" in front of sentences with transitive verbs and "I" in front of sentences with intransitive verbs. Underline each verb twice; for each transitive verb, circle the direct object. The first one has been done for you.

___T___ **1.** Students sometimes set off fire alarms by accident.

______ **2.** Yesterday's alarm rang for five minutes.

______ **3.** The principal gave specific instructions over the P.A.

______ **4.** Students and teachers placed their books on their desks.

_______ 5. Teachers hurriedly ushered students into the hall.

_______ 6. They counted the students as they left the classroom.

_______ 7. Out in the hall, smoke poured from the ductwork.

_______ 8. Surprisingly, nobody panicked.

_______ 9. The students followed directions carefully.

_______ 10. They filed out to their designated areas.

_______ 11. Students had learned good habits from previous fire drills.

_______ 12. The fire was burning in one of the shop classes.

_______ 13. A student had started a lawn mower with the gas cap off.

_______ 14. Gasoline spilled onto the engine and burst into flames.

_______ 15. The fire spread quickly.

_______ 16. Some students felt a burning sensation in their eyes.

_______ 17. They heard sirens from the street.

_______ 18. A rescue vehicle arrived at the same time as the fire truck.

_______ 19. Firefighters hurried into the building.

_______ 20. The fire was soon extinguished, but by then most of the school was filled with smoke.

Next Step Some verbs, such as *break, freeze,* and *sing,* can be either transitive or intransitive. Choose one of those verbs and write a sentence using it as a transitive verb. Then write another sentence using it as an intransitive verb.

Verbals

Verbals have split personalities—they are words that are part verb and part noun or adjective or adverb. For example, add *ing* to a verb, and it can become a **gerund**—a verb used as a noun. Or add *ing* or *ed* to a verb, and it can become a **participle**—a verb used as an adjective. Or introduce a verb with the word *to* and it becomes an **infinitive**—a verb used as either a noun, an adjective, or an adverb. (See 730.2–730.4 in *Write Source* for more information.)

Examples

Gerund:

Watching an expert play is a good way to improve your game.
("Watching" is used as a noun and the subject of the sentence.)

Participle:

The cat played a watching game with the confused mouse.
("Watching" and "confused" are used as adjectives. "Watching" modifies "game." "Confused" modifies "mouse.")

Infinitive:

To watch is to wait.
("To watch" is the subject and "to wait" is the predicate noun.)

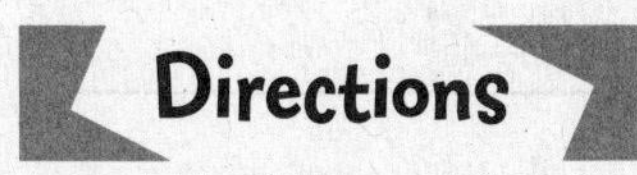

Underline the verbals in the sentences that follow. In the space below the sentence, name the type of verbal you have found, and explain the job it is doing. There may be more than one verbal in each sentence. The first sentence has been done for you.

1. Smirking at a teacher who scolds you is not wise.

   "Smirking" is a gerund used as the subject of the sentence.

2. Rewarding a dog with treats is a good training technique.

   ____

   ____

   ____

3. Trained elephants perform regularly so that they do not become restless.

4. I've always dreamed of acting in a broadway musical.

5. I would like to fly like a bird.

6. To win the next three games is the team's goal.

7. In most sports, timing is everything.

8. Applying for a passport is a good idea even if you don't have immediate travel plans.

Next Step Write three sentences following the direction given for each verbal: (1) Use *laughing* as an adjective, (2) use *walking* as a subject, and (3) use *to play* as a direct object. Now label each verbal as either a gerund, a participle, or an infinitive.

Types of Adjectives

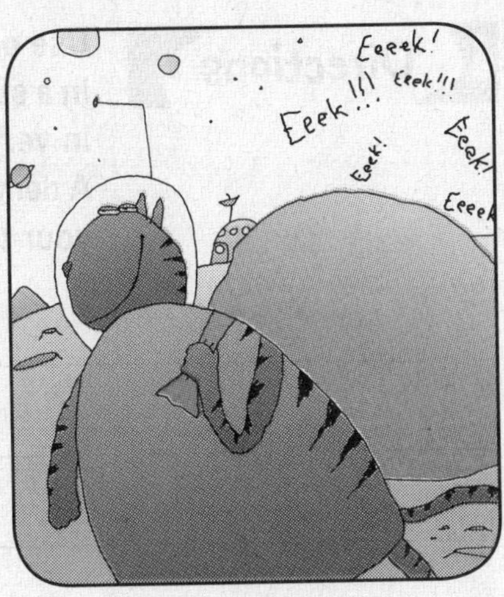

There are four special kinds of adjectives. They are demonstrative, compound, indefinite, and predicate. (See 732.4, 732.5, 734.1, and 734.2 in *Write Source* for help with this exercise.)

Directions **Each sentence has a different type of adjective underlined. In the space beneath each sentence, identify and then provide an explanation for each type.**

1. Some cats enjoy having many mice around.

   Type: ______________________________

   Explanation: An ______________ adjective is one that ______________

   ____

2. This kitten is mean, but that cat is meaner.

   Type: ______________________________

   Explanation: ______________________________

   ____

3. Scar-faced Bronty is no scaredy-cat guard.

   Type: ______________________________

   Explanation: ______________________________

   ____

4. A frustrated kitten is unpleasant and unpredictable.

   Type: ______________________________

   Explanation: ______________________________

   ____

Directions Use one of the four types of adjectives as one of the central characters in a story. An indefinite adjective, for example, might only think or speak in very general terms. Its favorite phrase might be "Gee, I'm not sure." A demonstrative adjective, on the other hand, might be very bossy. (Ask your teacher if you may work in pairs for this activity.)

Next Step Share your stories in your writing groups or with your class as a whole. Pay special attention to each adjective's personality.

Compound Adjectives

The screen door slams. Three-year-old Pooki runs into the kitchen and rummages through cabinets, asking, "Where is my zoo-buggy house?"

I hand my little neighbor the screen-topped "bug zoo" we made for catching fireflies. Pooki combines simple words she knows into picture-perfect descriptions without batting an eye.

Compound adjectives—two simple words linked as one compound word—are fun to use and, in informal writing, fun to invent. (See 732.5 in *Write Source* for more information.)

Examples

The fun-loving friends played kickball at the park.
("Kickball" always appears as one word; "fun-loving" doesn't.)

five-dollar bill **second-story office** **40-something years**
(Numbers combined with words to form compound adjectives are hyphenated.)

The old sock collector paid 50 dollars for hand-knitted argyles.
(Was the collector old? Then write "old sock-collector." Or was he a collector of old socks? If so, write "old-sock collector.")

Write compound adjectives in the blanks below. The first blank has been done for you. If you need help thinking of compound words, check out the word bank on the next page.

I will never forget the crazy, ___*goofed-up*___ Halloween party my sister and I threw for our ______________ friends. When the ______________ kids started arriving around 6:00 p.m., things looked normal. Within hours, though, everything changed.

We had the party in our ______________ barn. There was just one ______________ problem: my sister's ______________ donkey.

George, the donkey, doesn't move out of his ______________ stall unless it is his idea. So our ______________ plan was to include him in the party. George would be a steed in ______________ armor. Instead of bobbing for apples, our ______________ guests would hop on George and ride toward a ______________ scarecrow. The winner would have to knock the scarecrow's ______________ head off with a ______________ duster. It sounded simple.

We didn't anticipate George's ______________ enthusiasm for acting. Instead of aiming for the scarecrow, George headed for the ______________ refreshment table. As he slammed into the sawhorses supporting the tabletop, soda pop cans burst and sprayed sticky fountains at the ______________ lights. The lights went out.

Shrieking kids crowded toward the door of the ______________ barn. There, they ran smack into a ______________ phantom with burning eyes! Was it a ______________ monster? Nope. It was our ______________ tractor covered with ______________ paint!

goofed-up	**happy-go-lucky**	**bullheaded**	**straw-stuffed**	**blacked-out**
glow-in-the-dark	**seventh-grade**	**30-some**	**cleaned-up**	**fire-breathing**
overhead	**so-called**	**pumpkin-head**	**makeshift**	**teeny-weeny**
lawn-mower	**well-decorated**	**tinfoil**	**lambs-wool**	**warm-up**
snaggletoothed	**oversized**	**half-baked**	**fun-loving**	**noise-making**

Predicate Adjectives

You know that an adjective tells something special about a noun. The noun a predicate adjective describes is always the subject of a sentence or a clause. Predicate adjectives are easy to spot, too, because they always follow a linking verb.

"Wait a minute," you're thinking. "Predicate nouns follow linking verbs, too!" Indeed, they do—but predicate nouns rename the subject instead of describing it. (See 734.2 in *Write Source* for more information.)

Examples

Predicate Adjective:

The future is predictable in science fiction.

(The verb "is" links the subject noun "future" to its predicate adjective "predictable.")

Predicate Noun:

***Aliens* is a science-fiction movie about the future.**

(The verb "is" links the subject "*Aliens*" to the predicate noun "movie.")

Note: Most **linking verbs** are forms of the verb *be—am, is, are, was, were, be, being, been*. Other verbs—*smell, feel, look, taste, remain, appear, sound, seem, become, grow, stand,* and *turn*—may also do the job of linking a subject to a predicate noun or a predicate adjective. Some words may be used as both linking verbs and action verbs. How the verb functions in a *particular* sentence is the key to whether it is a linking verb or an action verb.

In the sentences below, underline the subject once and the verb twice. Then label each bold-faced word: "PA" for predicate adjective or "PN" for predicate noun. The first one has been done for you.

1. People are **curious** about finding new ways to build houses. (PA)
2. A house may not look any **different** from its neighbor, but its building blocks may be **extraordinary!**
3. Straw-bale houses are grand **properties** or simple **huts.**
4. The laziest one of the *Three Little Pigs* was not the first **builder** to decide that straw is an excellent construction **material.**

5. Houses of compacted straw coated with clay were **common** in ancient Asia and Europe.

6. A one-room schoolhouse built in 1886 near Bayard, Nebraska, is the first recorded **building** made of rectangular bales.

7. An article in a book titled *Shelter* is **responsible** for renewed interest in straw-bale building.

8. Straw houses coated with stucco, plaster, or clay look **beautiful** and are very **strong.**

9. The houses are unusually **well-insulated.**

10. Straw is an abundant and a renewable **resource.**

11. Air in a straw house is generally **free** of fumes and pollutants.

12. Building with bales is **speedy;** walls can be erected in one weekend.

13. Houses built of straw are still **rare**—but they can be found from the United States to Russia, and from France to Nova Scotia and Mexico.

Next Step Read about other unusual kinds of houses in other books at your library. Let your imagination run wild! Write a description of your ideal house in your journal. Use some colorful predicate adjectives.

Forms of Adjectives

An adjective is used to describe a noun or a pronoun—"the *small* TV." An adjective can even go one step further when it is used in a comparison—"the TV is *smaller* than your fist." Each adjective has three forms of comparison: *positive, comparative*, and *superlative.* (See the examples below and 734.3–734.5 in *Write Source* for more information.)

Examples

Positive:

Frozen yogurt is a light dessert. It is delicious.
(The *positive form* of an adjective describes a noun or a pronoun without comparing it to anyone or anything else.)

Comparative:

Frozen yogurt is a lighter dessert than ice cream.
Frozen yogurt is more delicious than ice cream.
(The *comparative form* of an adjective [adjective + *er*] compares two nouns or pronouns. Most adjectives of two or more syllables use the modifier "more," instead of adding *er,* to show the comparison.)

Superlative:

Frozen yogurt is the lightest dessert of the five on this menu.
Frozen yogurt is the most delicious dessert I can think of.
(The *superlative form* of an adjective [adjective + *est*] compares three or more nouns or pronouns. Most adjectives of two or more syllables use the modifier "most," instead of adding *est,* to show the comparison.)

Note: A few adjectives are irregular (*good, better, best* and *little, less, least*).

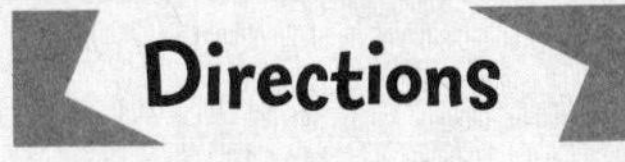

Use each of the following adjectives in a sentence. Use the adjective in the form indicated in parentheses. The first one has been done for you.

tall **1.** At 20,320 feet, Mt. McKinley is ___tall___ (*positive*), while South America's Mt. Aconcagua is even ___taller___ (*comparative*), but Mt. Everest is the ___tallest___ (*superlative*).

old 2. Evan, born at 11:59 p.m. on July 3, is a day ____________ than
(comparative)
his twin brother, born at 12:04 a.m. on July 4.

funny 3. Who is the ____________ comedian on television?
(superlative)

good 4. I am good at all of the "extreme-B" sports—boards, blades, and BMX biking—but I am ____________ at snowboarding.
(superlative)

charming 5. The only quality my mom finds ____________ in a
(comparative)
daughter than whining is the ability to burp on command.

good 6. You can buy many types of tires for a road bike, but for traction on dry pavement, the ____________ tire has no tread, so its
(superlative)
surface is totally in contact with the road.

comfortable 7. My dad's recliner is really ugly, but it is ____________
(comparative)
than my mom's rocking chair.

boring 8. That picnic was so ____________ that even the mosquitoes
(positive)
fell asleep, but it was not the ____________ picnic I've
(superlative)
ever attended.

bad 9. My brother got a ____________ grade in ninth-grade
(positive)
algebra, but my grade was ____________.
(comparative)

Next Step As you completed the activity above, you probably noticed that some adjectives like *bad, worse,* and *worst* are irregular. Compare notes with your classmates and see how many irregular adjectives you can think of.

Adverbs

Adverbs are used to modify verbs, adjectives, or other adverbs. There are four basic types of adverbs: *adverbs of time, place, manner,* and *degree.* (See page 736 in *Write Source* for more information.)

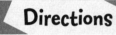

Directions **Circle 11 adverbs in the following sentences. The first sentence has been done for you.**

1. Lightning streaked continuously, driving jagged spears into the dark night.
2. John's mother hesitantly and shakily agreed that the lightning was pretty.
3. Four-year-old John found the whole experience quite exciting.
4. Suddenly, they were plunged into darkness.
5. To move in the dark was very difficult, but they slowly managed to find their way.
6. The first thing that they spotted was a brightly flashing red light.
7. Cars were moving slowly as they approached the corner.
8. John and his mother walked cautiously across the street.
9. They stepped carefully onto the curb.
10. John and his mother will never forget that experience.

Next Step Write four more adverbs on the lines below. Then use all five adverbs in sentences in a very short story.

especially __________ __________

__________ __________ __________

Directions In the space below, write a descriptive paragraph about drivers of cars or motorcycles and how they maneuver through traffic. Use each of the listed adverbs in the paragraph.

well fast quickly often entirely

Forms of Adverbs

An adverb is a word that tells us more about a verb, an adjective, or another adverb. Adverbs usually explain *how, when, where,* or *to what extent (how often, how long, how much)* something happened.

They have three forms: positive, comparative, and superlative. The positive form modifies another word without making a comparison. (See 738.2–738.4 in *Write Source* for more information.)

Examples

Positive:

Performing fleas train vigorously.
("Vigorously" modifies the verb "train" without making any comparisons.)

Comparative:

Jumping frogs train more vigorously than performing fleas.
("More vigorously" modifies the verb "train" and compares how "frogs" train to how "fleas" train.)

Superlative:

Fido's flea is the most vigorously trained insect in the world.
("Most vigorously" modifies the adjective "trained" and compares one "flea" to all other insects.)

Use each of the following words as an adverb in a sentence. (Use the adverb in the form indicated in parentheses.) The first one has been done for you.

bad **1.** When the teacher stepped out of the room, the students behaved *badly* . *(positive)*

clear **2.** Greg speaks ________________ *(comparative)* than Ann, his opponent for student council.

fast **3.** Who ran ________________ *(superlative)* in the relay?

gentle **4.** She ________________ *(positive)* stroked the frightened dog.

noisy **5.** Mark my words, this discussion began quietly, but it will end

__________.
(positive)

careful **6.** Lock the door __________—__________
(positive) *(comparative)*

than you have ever done it before!

loud **7.** Marshmallow Man from *Ghostbusters* stomps around

__________.
(positive)

quick **8.** He won the pancake-eating contest by floating the flapjacks in milk and gulping them __________.
(superlative)

sincere **9.** Think carefully about the questions, and answer them

__________.
(positive)

stylish **10.** The '57 Thunderbird sports car was designed __________
(comparative)

than that year's Chevy Corvette model, but the Chevy has become a legend.

well **11.** Picabo Street skied __________ in the 1998 Winter Olympics,
(superlative)

even though she was recovering from a serious injury.

slow **12.** Please drive __________!
(positive)

Next Step Now you try it! Write three sentences about a game or contest. Write one sentence in which you use one adverb in the positive form, one in the comparative form, and one in the superlative form.

Prepositions

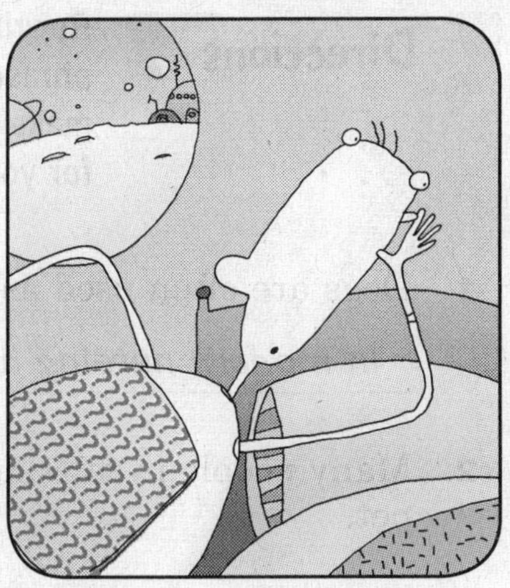

Prepositions such as *at, about, by, for, in, of, on,* and *to,* among others, have been used in our language for well over 1,400 years. Prepositions are words that show position or direction. They also introduce prepositional phrases.

Prepositional phrases are an indispensable part of our language. (*Indispensable* means we can't do without them.) Just think how sentences, such as the examples below, would read without the prepositional phrases. There wouldn't be much left, would there? (See page 742 in *Write Source* for more information.)

Examples

Prepositional Phrases:

Write every day in a personal journal.

Begin writing with a particular idea in mind.

Underline all of the prepositional phrases in the journal entry below. *Caution:* Do not underline infinitives (the word "to" followed by a verb) as prepositional phrases! The first one has been done for you.

April 12

I was late for my guitar lesson tonight. Usually, I'm at the studio by 6:30, but I was late because of my cat Tom. He ran away during last night's storm. I looked everywhere for him.

I looked in the garage because there are lots of little niches in there. I looked in the laundry room because cats usually like to curl up in warm, soft places. I finally headed outside and even looked in the trees. Tom just wasn't to be found, so I stopped looking. After supper, I heard a purr in my room. Leave it to a cat to be unpredictable. I found Tom under the bed.

Directions Rewrite the following sentences so that each begins with a prepositional phrase. Place a comma after the phrase if you think one is needed to make the meaning of the sentence clear. The first one has been done for you.

1. Dogs are often used as companions in modern nursing homes.

   In modern nursing homes, dogs are often used as companions.

2. Many people in nursing homes think of the resident dog as their very own pet.

3. Some residents leave out special treats for the dog's daily visit.

4. Golden retrievers are suitable pets according to some staff members.

5. The nurses usually walk the dogs between shifts.

Next Step Write a story starter, similar to the one below, using a two-word preposition from the list on page 742 in *Write Source*. (Share your results.)

> **Together with** **her friend, Elisha was a curious young lady. One foggy September evening, her curiosity led to . . .**

Interjections

An interjection is a word or phrase used to express strong emotion or surprise. *Wow!* and *Yikes!* are interjections. A comma or an exclamation point is usually used to separate the interjection from the rest of the sentence. (See page 746 in *Write Source* for more information.)

Directions **Underline each interjection in the sentences that follow. The first one has been done for you.**

1. "Hey, Joe, guess where I'm going next week?"
2. "Well, let's see," answered Joe. "To Australia? Siberia? The moon?"
3. "Okay, enough of the wise-guy routine. I'm going scuba diving."
4. "Cool. Do you get to use air tanks and all that?" asked Joe.
5. "Yep, and we get to explore a coral reef and a couple of shipwrecks."
6. "Holy mackerel! That sounds like a great time. Do you need someone to carry your flippers or something?" asked Joe, drooling.
7. "Oops, I forgot to sign up for flippers. Thanks for reminding me."
8. "What kind of creatures do you expect to see? I mean, whoa, you better stay away from the sharks, barracudas, and octopuses," warned Joe.
9. "Yeah, I'll keep my distance. Hmmm, maybe I should buy some shark repellent or something."
10. "Nah," Joe laughed. "No shark is going to be interested in someone as tasteless as you!"

Directions On the lines below, write your own dialogue about an adventure you've had (or would like to have). Use interjections whenever they seem right. If they are used well, interjections will make your dialogue sound much more real.

Subordinating Conjunctions

Subordinating conjunctions connect clauses to form complex sentences. The resulting complex sentences often carry more meaning than the shorter independent clauses and also help to make your writing read more smoothly. (See 746.1 in *Write Source* for more information.)

Examples

Two Sentences:
Martha entered a 124-mile ice-skating race. She felt ready for it.

A Compound Sentence:
Martha entered a 124-mile ice-skating race, and she felt ready for it.
(A comma and the coordinating conjunction "and" connect the two sentences.)

A Complex Sentence:
Martha entered a 124-mile ice-skating race because she felt ready for it.
(The subordinating conjunction "because" connects the two sentences.)

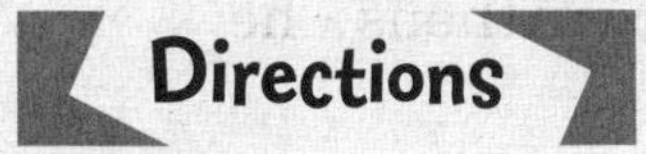

Subordinating conjunctions connect two ideas to form meaningful complex sentences. Some subordinating conjunctions express time (*before*), some express the reason why (*because*), and some serve as conditional words (*unless*). In each of the sentences, circle the subordinating conjunctions. Put the group of words (or clause) each conjunction introduces in parentheses. The first one has been done for you.

1. For his own safety, a soccer referee in Greece disguised himself as a priest after a match because (he had greatly upset the local fans).
2. Alex Wickham must have had a lot of confidence since he dove from a rocky cliff the height of a 20-story building.
3. He lost consciousness before he hit the water.
4. Although he survived the dive, his body was all black-and-blue.

5. Two tennis players once continued a point for 78 straight minutes until one player had to stop the volley to give a tennis lesson.

6. When Lawson Robertson and Harry Hillman set a track-and-field record, they did it in a three-legged race.

7. Although he had a 150-pound man on his back, Noah Young ran a mile in 8 minutes 30 seconds.

8. While Ernest Mensen ran a distance of 1,960 miles, he ate only biscuits covered with raspberry syrup.

9. Ernest Mensen saved time when he ran because he knew how to find shortcuts through forests.

10. The modern marathon race got its name from the plain of Marathon in Greece where an ancient battle took place.

11. When a man named Philippedes ran from Marathon to Athens, he delivered the news of a Greek victory over Persia.

12. Because the first marathon was 26 miles, the modern marathon race during the Olympic Games is also 26 miles.

Next Step Write a paragraph about a cooking, camping, or classroom experience. Use short, simple sentences as if you were just learning to read and write. Then exchange paragraphs with a classmate and revise each other's work. Try to use some subordinate conjunctions in your revisions.

Coordinating and Correlative Conjunctions

The place two roads come together is called a *junction.* A similar word *conjunction* is the name of the part of speech that joins things—other words, phrases, or clauses. There are three types of conjunctions. This exercise will look at two of the three types: coordinating and correlative. **Coordinating conjunctions** always connect two equal sentence elements of the same kind—a word to a word, a phrase to a phrase, or a clause to a clause. **Correlative conjunctions,** like coordinating conjunctions, connect elements of the same kind, but correlative conjunctions are used in pairs. (See page 744 in *Write Source* for more information.)

Examples

Coordinating Conjunction:

Mathematics and music communicate without language.
(The coordinating conjunction "and" connects two words—"mathematics" and "music.")

Correlative Conjunction:

Choose either music or art as your elective class.
(The correlative conjunctions "either," "or" connect two words—"music" and "art.")

Join each pair of sentences that follow using coordinating or correlative conjunctions. You may delete words and move words around. The first sentence has been done for you.

1. I would like to visit Iceland. I would also like to visit Greenland.

   I would like to visit Iceland and Greenland.

2. In high school, I want to try out for track. I also want to try out for basketball.

   ____

   ____

3. Many athletes want to play two sports. The seasons have to be at different times.

   ____

   ____

4. In some places football and soccer have the same season. A student must choose one sport or the other.

5. My brother could not decide which sport to play. He had to choose football or soccer.

6. He enjoys both sports. He's pretty good at football and soccer.

7. He finally chose football. He was happy to have made a decision.

8. He was unhappy about missing his friends on the soccer team. He also thought he would miss the constant movement and pace of a soccer game.

9. Now he talks about football all the time. We used to talk together about both soccer and football.

Parts of Speech Review 1

In the English language there are eight parts of speech. They help you understand words and how to use them. Every word in every sentence is a part of speech.

Directions **Write one of the eight parts of speech under each of the eight faces. If you need help, turn to page 748 in *Write Source*. Then write a sentence that uses that part of speech on the blank beside the face. Circle the word.**

Directions Identify the part of speech for each underlined word. Find five examples of each part of speech, except for the interjection, which has only one example. (Look at page 748 in *Write Source*.)

nouns	☐ ☐ ☐ ☐ ☐	adverbs	☐ ☐ ☐ ☐ ☐	conjunctions	☐ ☐ ☐ ☐ ☐
verbs	☐ ☐ ☐ ☐ ☐	adjectives	☐ ☐ ☐ ☐ ☐	interjection	☐
pronouns	☐ ☐ ☐ ☐ ☐	prepositions	☐ ☐ ☐ ☐ ☐		

In the summer after eighth grade, Rene took a bus from Vermont to her uncle's cottage in New Jersey. Her "graduation present" turned out to be a crash course in the school of life.

At a stop in New York City, she visited a newsstand. Suddenly, someone snatched her purse. She never saw the thief. Her ticket and her money were gone. She patted her side as if the bag would reappear. Anger overwhelmed her. Oh, how could someone be so evil? How would she get to Ocean City now?

Fortunately, the bus driver let her call her parents. They told her about Western Union, the nationwide telegraph network. Her parents promised to wire money to the nearest agent.

Hiking through downtown Manhattan, she composed herself. In high school, she would write a fine story about her adventure. In the cramped Western Union office, she studied people with a writer's eye. They looked tired and afraid. Everyone there had a problem. But when a man beside her in a tie-dyed T-shirt started to whistle, everybody laughed. They became a kind of family.

Later, while she was sunning herself on the Jersey shore, she decided her story would not be about crime. It would be about the feelings and experiences that draw people together.

Parts of Speech Review 2

Directions Unscramble the words below to name the eight parts of speech.

1. unno ____________ (6)
2. berv ____________ (6)
3. spotiperion ____________ (6)
4. ropnoun ____________ (6)
5. tadviejec ____________ (6)
6. brevda ____________ (6)
7. junconontic ____________ (6)
8. jecretnition ____________ (1)

Directions Identify the part of speech for each underlined word. The number after each scrambled word above tells you how many examples of that part of speech are underlined in the exercise. (See page 748 in *Write Source*.)

You would recognize Robin Williams or Danny DeVito on TV. But would you recognize a picture of the most famous cartoon-voice actor in history, the man who created over 500 different voices?

The man with the rubber voice was Mel Blanc. You know him as Bugs Bunny and Foghorn Leghorn, as Yosemite Sam and the Tasmanian Devil, as Fred Flintstone and Porky Pig—to name just a few of the hundreds of characters he created for Warner Brothers. During the glory days of radio, Blanc performed weekly in 18 transcontinental radio shows. He also commanded top pay when recording for rival companies, once earning $800 for Gideon the Cat's hiccup in the Disney movie *Pinocchio.* (At the time, other cartoon actors were earning a mere $50 a day.)

Blanc started his career as a musician and bandleader. Luckily for us, one evening in the 1930s he was asked to host a talent show in Portland,

Oregon. A blizzard forced the contestants to stay home.

Blanc decided to do the entire show himself! He cleverly created a voice for each of the "contestants"—a yodeler, a violinist, and a hillbilly—and faked interviews with them, using his "real" voice as the interviewer. The audience loved him.

After his surprising success, Blanc headed for Hollywood. Getting an audition with a cartoon company was not easy. For a year and a half, Warner Brothers refused to hear him. His lucky break came when the studio needed a new voice for a drunken bull.

About that time, Warner Brothers was developing the character of a timid little pig. When Blanc was asked in a interview if he had lived on a farm, he replied, "No, but I went out to a pig farm and wallowed around for a couple of weeks." That is how Porky Pig got his voice.

Around that time, Bugs Hardaway was developing another new character. He described Happy Rabbit as little, tough, and a real stinker. Mel Blanc thoughtfully remarked that the toughest voice in the United States had to be from the Bronx or Brooklyn. Blanc easily combined the New York accents and then suggested that Happy Rabbit's name should be changed to honor his creator. Thus, Bugs Bunny was born.

Sylvester the Cat got a very slurpy sounding voice because he is a sloppy-looking cat. Daffy Duck's voice is a lot like Sylvester's but was recorded at a different speed. Because he is tiny, Tweety got a baby voice. Even Woody Woodpecker, who was performed by Walter Lanz, owes his trademark laugh to Mel Blanc.